THE ECSTASY OF CABEZA DE VACA

BY KEITH HILL

POETRY
The Lounging Lizard Poet of the Floating World

CLASSICS OF WORLD MYSTICISM
The Bhagavad Gita: A New Poetic Version
I Cannot Live Without You:
Selected Poetry of Mirabai and Kabir
Interpretations of Desire:
Mystic Love Poems by the Sufi Master Ibn 'Arabi
Psalms of Exile and Return

FICTION
Puck of the Starways
Blue Kisses

NON-FICTION
The New Mysticism
The God Revolution
Striving To Be Human

THE ECSTASY OF CABEZA DE VACA

Keith Hill

First published in 2015 by Disjunct Books
Auckland, New Zealand

Paperback ISBN 978-0-473-32407-0

Cover image: Juanjo Tugore / Shutterstock

Disjunct Books is an imprint of Attar Books, a New Zealand
publisher focused on spiritually oriented literature. For more
information on Disjunct Books' publications visit:

www.attarbooks.com

Contents

Preface | 7

1   Landfall | 13
2   The Drifting Canoe | 20
3   A Necklace Of Bones | 26
4   Cannibals Near Kill Us | 33
5   My Captivity Begins | 40
6   The Devouring Web | 50
7   From Hope To Despair | 60
8   Tasting With Butterflies | 70
9   I Am Saved By Shells | 75
10   A Miscellany Of Customs | 81
11   Escape Is Delayed | 88
12   Fields Of Spikes | 99
13   The Burning Tree | 109
14   A Buried Arrowhead | 118
15   We Eat Dog And Depart | 125
16   A New Custom Arises | 131
17   Flying Among Eagles | 137
18   A Dead Man Walks | 148
19   The Destitute Plain | 154
20   A Christian Welcome | 163
21   The Glowing Jungle | 171

Preface

THIS NARRATIVE RECOUNTS the extraordinary adventures of Alvar Núñez Cabeza de Vaca, who in June 1527 left Spain as treasurer and second-in-command of an expedition to the New World. Led by Pánfilo de Narváez, the expedition's goal was to claim Florida for the Spanish crown, establish towns and armed garrisons, convert the native Indians to Christianity, and find treasure and gold to reward the expedition's backers and pay a premium to the King.

In August 1527 five vessels carrying six hundred men arrived in Santo Domingo in the Dominican Republic. One hundred immediately deserted. Then, when Narváez sent two vessels commanded by Cabeza de Vaca and Captain Pantoja to Trinidad to collect fresh supplies and find replacement men, they were struck by a hurricane. The vessels sank, sixty men drowned, and the purchased stores were lost.

Eventually, in April 1528, over four hundred men sailing five vessels reached the coast of modern day Tampa Bay. The expedition quickly lost its way. One ship was lost, another sent to find safe harbour never returned. A ship sent to Cuba to replenish stores spent a year attempting to find Narváez and his men, without success.

Accident and misfortune soon compounded to disaster. After a storm forced the colonisers onto the shore, a trek inland in search of the gold found no treasure but resulted in many deaths. When yet more storms sank the expedition's remaining ships the survivors built four rafts. De Vaca urged that the rafts be lashed together, but Narváez decided not. Surging tides and winds soon separated the rafts. Narváez and those with him were never seen again. Thereafter forty survivors were reduced by slavery, starvation, disease and random acts of Indian cruelty. Eight years later only four men remained alive. They arrived in Mexico City, having walked from the Gulf of Mexico to the Pacific coast.

We know what happened because Cabeza de Vaca wrote two accounts of his adventures, the first published in 1542, the second in 1555. Appended to the later account was de Vaca's view of the misunderstandings and deceit that played out when he was in charge of Spain's colony in Buenos Aires in the early 1540s. Cabeza de Vaca likely died in Seville in 1558, impoverished and unacknowledged.

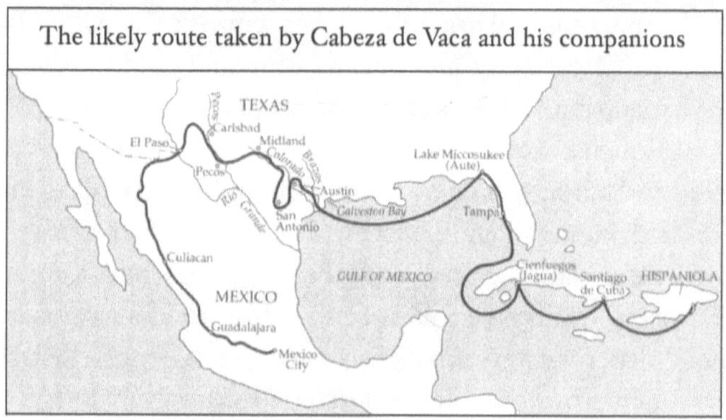

I first read Cabeza de Vaca's adventure in 1977. A number of details make his story remarkable. His is the ultimate surviv-al story. Yet despite the tremendous trials he went through with his fellow survivors, there is no trace of self-pity in de Vaca's account. Rather, he remained totally grounded in the world in which he found himself. In fact, he so closely observed Indian culture, and so accurately recorded what he witnessed, that his work is acknowledged today as the first European ethnographic account of Central American tribespeople and their customs.

Psychologically, de Vaca's account of his journey reflects the growth of his understanding. When he first arrived in the New World his view of the native population reflected the then prevailing European view that the Indians were savages to be feared and exploited. But asa result of living among them, Cabeza de Vaca's perspective changed radically. In particular, his stand against taking slaves is exceptional in an era when Christopher Columbus and the rampaging conquistadors who followed him, notably Hernán Cortés, the conquerer of the Aztecs, and Francisco Pizarro, who dismantled the Inca Empire, treated the indigenous peoples with heartless cruelty.

Finally, there is the spiritual journey that Cabeza de Vaca and his companions made. Scholars have compared what de Vaca went through to Lear's journey of self-discovery, in which the king was stripped of his power, identity, status, and, in the end, sanity. Cabeza de Vaca's inner transformation was equally extreme. He first lost his mission, then his freedom, his clothing, and his standing as a human being. But after being inwardly eviscerated he discovered other resources within, including miraculous powers, and a new appreciation of humanity and the world. Whether God was responsible, as de Vaca himself believed, or whether what he went through was a variety of transpersonal transformation, he emerged from his eight-year ordeal like a butterfly from its chrysalis, utterly changed.

However, there is one central problem with Cabeza de Vaca's account. It lacks self-reflection. He offers no insights into his feelings and thoughts. How did he cope with the deaths of his fellow Spaniards? With being enslaved? To what extent did his experiences cause his values to progressively shift, and his view of his religion and its God to change?

On these questions, and on much else of a personal nature that we today regard as essential to any telling of a life story, de Vaca is silent. But I wanted to know more. I wanted to enter more deeply into Cabeza de Vaca. De Vaca not being here to transport us into his inner world, I decided to do so myself. This book is the result. It is offered from Cabeza de Vaca's perspective, being written in the final years of his life as he looks back at his remarkable adventure.

I commence this retelling with the words the aging ad-
venturer might have written to preface this final account of
the most significant years of his life:

This is the testimony of a man who departed Spain in
the year of our Lord 1527, in the position of treasurer to
an expedition to the New World, and did return in 1537,
forever changed.

For some these pages shall read as the over-wrought
testimony of a civilised man made delirious by his
exposure to the crude beliefs and practices of savages.
Yet be certain that what is reported here is offered
soberly and honestly, and is projected in accordance
with his powers from the shaken heart of his journey.

This witness to his own unanticipated adventure
can do no more than testify that the intoxicating,
the ecstatic, and the over-reaching, no less than the
customary, God-fearing, and sanctioned, do truly lie on
a path that stretches, one step at a time, from this spot
to the very portals of heaven, which are not as far from
us as we are taught to believe.

Alvar Núñez Cabeza de Vaca, Seville, 1557

THE ECSTASY OF
CABEZA DE VACA

1 Landfall

WE SURGED from the sea
ecstatic, demented
sagged on the still swaying shore
our cracked mouths filled with joy.

Five days we prayed for this
feared it would never come
that devouring death
which hovered over our swaying hopes
which filled our one sail with despair
blowing our broken raft this way, that
would feed us eventually to the deep
and there all our hopes would drown.
Now we felt firm land beneath our cheeks.
And as the tide nuzzled our beards
sucked backwards
pulled streaming sand across wrinkled hands
we raised our heads
dumbly stared into each others' eyes
and knew there was a God.
That, ultimately, all was good.

> "Our Father, which are in heaven
> to You we make a shameful confession:
> we feared this day would never come."

Seven men we were in number
kneeled, in a circle, shoulder to shoulder
bewildered
trembling
terrified

scarce strong enough to hold ourselves erect.
Seven battered heads bowed in a rasp of prayer:

>"To You who are a mystery
>whose measures are unfathomable
>here and now we give thanks
>contented with the workings of Your will
>until our time itself should end.
>Through Jesus Christ, our Lord. Amen."

That "Amen" echoed in seven chastened hearts.
Then, as one, we turned our eyes
towards the land that had proved our ark.
In the darkening light of dusk
we saw a glowing stretch of sand
and a dank wall of jungle leaves.
Birds sang within, life quickening life
promising food and the luxury of shelter.
All we saw was another deep in which
who knows what terrors lurked.
No words passed that moment between us.
But, as one, we turned back towards the sea.

Θ Θ Θ

Man is not man without fire.
We squatted like savages
eating beach grasses
reduced as we had been by our days at sea
to that primeval state we shared
with Adam in the garden.
Except he never needed fire
being radiated by God.
And except our innocence was long lost.
I cannot speak for my emaciated men
but in my salt-wrinkled heart

and despite the savour of our prayer
I doubted we were yet saved.
All we were was not yet dead.
As we huddled together in the dark
no sleep came nor respite from our dread.
For while hard sand held our bodies firm
I could feel Leviathan sweeping the depths
that continued to sway beneath me
feeding the fear that we were abandoned
in our good God's true and just creation.

θ θ θ

A morning's laboured walk confirmed it.
Captain Andrés Dorantes was with me
a commonsense and courageous man
whose judgement the years had well burnished.
We tramped the lumped course of dunes
staggered where the curved shore led
often forced to stop, sit, draw deep breaths
so weak we were from our torment at sea.
Yet hours of sweat and aching stagger
but returned us to our makeshift raft:
we had beached on an island
and the jungle we had darkly feared last night
that it crawled with all palpable terrors
day revealed to be thin, straggling and safe.
No beasts threatened our survival.
We were where we had prayed to be.
Yet there was trouble in this too
for neither was there food.
The birds we disturbed by our walking
proved to be resting not feeding.
They circled the island crying
then flew out to sea.
We waited. They never did return.

Where did they fly to? Another shore?
We could but hope.
For given we would surely starve
if we made this island our final stop
that shore we knew nothing of
we had no choice but to assay.

ϴ ϴ ϴ

Half a day we creaked on the waves
praying wind and tide
would not pull us back to sea
too tired to row ourselves to safety
even if we knew its direction.
In truth, we were past despair
at the ocean's mercy
resigned to our God's chosen fate
when we saw a green line of tree-tops
that stood above the swelling ocean
and smoke drifting above all.
Our hearts leapt.
But hope is the cruellest emotion:
it most betrays when most heaven-sent.
For smoke meant men.
None spoke of our shared nightmare
yet each vividly knew what it was—
that we would fall in with the cannibals
we had heard the miseries of in Spain.
The most severe of this land's savages
would shatter our chests with adzes
wrest out our still throbbing hearts
throw them on the fire to roast
and suck the marrow from our bones
grinning at us all the while
we writhed our last moments of dying.
That I have written these fevered words

is witness to our unspoken fear.
That I am alive to write them now
proves how far our fear was a lie.
The truth is we fell exhausted and starved
onto a golden arc of sand.
We heard the screech of parakeets
felt the waves lap our legs
watched the breeze caress the jungle leaves
smelt the smoke drifting in the sunlight—
and felt the thud of stone striking wood.
If we had come to paradise to die
we were too broken to care.
We lay like morsels on our fractured raft
mesmerised by knowing men
we had long prayed would find and save us
worked now not far away
feeding the fire that could finish us all.
Yet was this to be our end?
Were we too starved to save the meagre flesh
that hung now from our starkened bones?
I, Cabeza de Vaca, was not!
This was not the paradise I sought of God.
Nor was it the paradise to claim me now.
A paddle my crutch
I levered my numb body to its feet
forced it to stagger up the slope of sand
and approached the wall of jungle.
I thrust my face into the leaves—
and was shocked to find a face peering back.
Startled, I pitched straight backwards
falling onto the hard daze of sand.

A savage face loomed over me.
Two grizzled men with bones
in their noses stood either side of it.
The day was darker and the air cooler

than I remembered from what
must have been but a moment before.
My men lay sprawled around me
drag marks in the sand
trailing back to the beached raft.
It seemed some time had passed
and we all were too stunned to stand.
A grunt focused my thoughts.
The looming savage bared his blackened teeth.
I watched him hold out his hand:
a wizened piece of charcoal
nested between his fingertips.
He pushed it up against my closed mouth
brought it back to his own blackened lips
and smacked them loudly.
Again he forced the charcoal against mine.
I felt it push up from deep inside me.
It squeezed past my chest
rose jaggedly into my throat
and forced my split lips open:
laughter—that I thought had died in me.
A cracked wheeze sounded from
the broken depths of my splintered heart.
The savages we feared would kill and eat us all
were giving us back our lives
by sharing food from their very mouths!

The charcoal lumps were slugs
the savages dug from rotting tree trunks
and cooked in coals before eating.
These soft and sweet grubs
provided our first meal of a month.
Four among us vomited what we ate.
Yet these lowly slugs revived us all.
When dawn arrived next morning
we had the strength to stand.

And think.
I talked apart with Dorantes
plotting a path out of this wilderness.
None of us was as rugged
as this untamed land or its fierce life.
Stay too long and we certainly would die.
So we hatched a plan.
Dorantes would take three:
his brother Diego, Figuero from Toledo
and the Moroccan Berber Estevanico.
That four would accompany our saviours
to their village which pointed fingers
showed was inland and northerly.
I would take the two remaining:
Captain Alonso del Castillo
and the callow youth Estrada.
We would trek southwards down the coast.
Each group would seek news of Christians.
We would meet in three moon's time
on this same sparkling wedge of sand
and share what we had discovered.
I confess I did not then hear
the steaming wilderness laugh
at our ignorance of the true reason
God had brought us to the world's edge.
And it would take more pain
more misery, ecstasy, horror
than any of us ever imagined to ...
My pen fails. Grant me leave.
That is all my tale for this day.

2   The Drifting Canoe

NINE DAYS we walked that coast.
Thirst drove us
into a delirium of dryness.
Lips cracked, tongues cleaved in our mouths.
Yet when we felt too weak to walk
we found what was just sufficient to survive:
brackish water in a fallen tree's hollow
a trickle of moisture
running from tree roots down a raw rock face
a beached dead fish we fought sea birds for
to pick the last flesh from its bones.
The eggs of a colony of nesting gannets
delayed us two days and nights
while we gorged ourselves to fullness
eating also the raw carcass of a bird we brained
with weakly thrown rocks.
Thus we fed our strength sufficiently to persist.

My one unshakable vow
made on the altar of my determined heart
was never to surrender
never to allow this gruelling wilderness
to grind us dust to dust.
My two companions were not as strong as me
but they were part now of my heart's promise
and I happily supplied the drive for three.
This is what a leader does:
he fights to place one foot, one body
one heart in front of the other
cajoling, pushing, demanding
to ensure our carcasses did not add to

the fated toll this coast took on its transients.
Such is the ignorance of man
that he apes authority and proclaims himself
a primate power over his fellow creatures
(even if his motive is protection and care)
when each man's projected will
is but one strand in the intertwined tracks
we tread through the world's troubled choices.
I had yet much to learn of what
truly chooses our course through life.
My first lesson occurred on the ninth day
of this our southward trek.

Θ Θ Θ

The river surprised us.
We rounded a headland and there it was:
a rippling muscle of water discharging
its fresh cargo into the salted sea.
My flagging companions abruptly transformed
as they shouted, ran and plunged into its surge.
We slaked our thirst for the first day
in our weeks of travails.
At such a time fresh water is ambrosia.
It takes but three lusty gulps
to make a man feel a god.
We immersed our sunburnt skin
salved our sweated faces
dissolved the salt from our hair
and joyed in what we saw
as a baptismal renewal of faith.

    "Lord, again we have cause
    to thank You for Your lavishing of care.
    We walk blindly through the world
    unlettered in the heavenly language

You have written on the world
to guide us to our soul's waystops.
Know, Lord, we ever praise but You
that each of our pain-filled steps
takes us nearer Your promised end."

Such, as I remember it, was Castillo's prayer
to which we gave our heartfelt "Amen".
Yet I saw young Estrada cast his gaze
downwards from the heavens
towards the head-bowed Castillo.
Fear, doubt and despair flashed
in a dismayed tumble across his face.
As we lifted ourselves from the water
I put an arm round his shoulders
and attempted to quell his disquiet.
Yet I confess I felt the force of his fear
wrap my own heart in a quail of anxiety.
Such is the frailty that makes us human.

The river brought us life
strength, hope—and a test.
My view was we follow the agreed plan
cross at the river's mouth
and continue our southward journey
in search of fellow Christians.
Castillo was for following the river
and drawing from the natives
what they knew of our lost companions.
Young Estrada took my side
yet due only to my rank of command.
At issue was water.
We lacked gourds and could find none
to carry the life-giving liquid with us.
If we walked from the river
and continued down the coast

would we be walking towards safety
or into doom by thirst?
Castillo was for following the river
that it would keep us refreshed.
Yet, I countered, when we found a village
which surely we would
that discovery could be the death of us.
In each direction, by river or coast
we faced possible salvation, likely slaughter.
The air was cooling when Castillo argued
we spend the night in prayer
and await the good Lord's sign.
At that very moment
Estrada shouted and held up a fish.
From a branch he had fashioned a spear
to hunt in the water grasses.
Three more fish soon followed.
Castillo proclaimed this a sign
that guidance on our course would follow.
Hunger ended our debate.

Θ Θ Θ

Overnight Estrada changed allegiance.
He had dreamed we walked the river.
Yet while that was sign enough for him
and he and Castillo now pressed me
to abandon my plan to continue south
I was not so disposed.
From what did my mulishness derive?
Was it my ambition to lead thwarted?
I saw I was now a leader
in my heart only, not in theirs.
Was I then reacting in pique?
Or was there some deeper premonition
leading to a position I could not rationalise

but that I intuited was true?
This was a question I would much return to
when faced by other choices
during the wrought years that followed.
For now, I could not in conscience agree.
So we three sat and waited.

The sign arrived at noon.
It was a canoe drifting on the river's current.
A Christian cross had been roped in place
where a man would sit to paddle.
My companions plunged into the water
but the current proved too swift
and their state too weakened
for them to capture it.
We three stood on the river's bank
observing mutely
as the drifting canoe bucked briefly
where the river's surge met a bar of sand
then bobbed out onto the sea
carrying its silent cross.
It turned slowly on the tide
then was drawn up the coast.
For a time the canoe and its cross
rose and fell on the waves.
Then it slid round a headland and was gone.

Ө Ө Ө

We sat in profound contemplation.
We had seen the sign we craved.
Yet what was its meaning?
Clearly Christians were, or had been, upriver.
But did those Christians yet remain there?
And were they living? Or dead?
Was the canoe a beckoning? Or a warning?

There was one way to answer these questions:
trek up river and learn for ourselves.
Yet for me this proposal remained troubling.
The undoubtable truth was
we were surrounded by the unknown
and the little we foresaw was that
whichever direction our feet walked
the only certainty was uncertainty.
Castillo mustered his view of the facts:
we had no means to carry water
on a trek southwards down the coast
whereas the river offered that necessity.
The canoe had given clear evidence
of which direction we should travel
in search of our lost companions
while the coast had given us no sign at all
but confirmation of our mortality.
He judged the river bank was our one choice.
I spent some time in silence.
I could not gainsay Castillo's logic.
All I had was an inexplicable feeling
the coast offered us more hope than the river.
Yet given that we had each held
none but inexplicable feelings since
we first clawed onto this inhospitable land
I could not but grimly nod.
We gathered our hopes and committed
our future to the roiling river
and the borderline safety of its banks.

3 A Necklace of Bones

FEAR preceded us
    making of each leaf rustle
each twig snap
even the innocent lapping at the shore
an occasion to pause
to deeply listen
and only after due caution
tentatively move on.
Multiplying our troubles
was our occasional need to walk inland
to bypass a tangle of tide-twisted roots
to round an inlet
or pass behind a rise where crumbling clay
pushed down to the river's edge.
Our caution duly intensified
as we stepped through wiry undergrowth
or picked our way between lowering trees
in any one of which might lurk our deaths.
Snagged by these hesitations
progress proved slow.

Yet there was in this something unexpected:
the world around us bloomed.
I felt a delicious sharpening of my senses.
Each sound, smell, vibration
the chirruping of birds
the scratching of insects
the unstoppable slurring of the river
the pumped wings of a startled bird
I experienced not as external to me
but instead as taking place within

as part of my inmost vitality.
All those days trekking the coast
we three talked of how alien we felt
walking an estranging land.
On our left heaved the ocean
across which waters roamed (we dreamed)
the lost vessels of our fleet seeking
the remnants of our ill-fated expedition.
Balancing this nominal safety was
the forest that thrust into us from our right
growling with threats and dangers.
So we walked the thin shrug of the shore
which provided but indifferent security.
Neither in safety nor directly menaced
we traversed an anxious border
in which the forested wilderness
remained a crawling threatening peril.
Yet having left the shore's unfeeling safety
crossed the threshold of our fear
and now entered the living jungle
to trace the river's sweeping surge
we were ourselves unneeded additions
to the wilderness' pulsing presence.
In this I felt it was not I
pushing into the wilderness
but rather that the wilderness penetrated me
making me feel within each moment of its life
a resonance so intense, so embracing
so overwhelming
it intoxicated my heart.
I have since come to consider this feeling was
the first hint of a transformation
God had long ago planned for me.
A transformation He now
inexorably lured me towards.

Θ Θ Θ

On the second day we found our men.
The first intimation was an oar.
Castillo spied it from a rise caught in reeds.
I waded out and dragged it to the bank.
Our spirits rose on reading the name
painted on its shaft: Santa Domingo.
This was the very vessel we had lost
a good three months since
as we sailed towards the wild Florida coast!
A sudden storm split two ships from our own.
We had neither seen nor heard
evidence of either ship until this day.
So our hopes understandably surged.
We next found a shredded shirt
then pantaloons I pulled from sucking mud.
My companions' cheers fell mute.
We walked in dread-growing silence.
That dread was confirmed by an arm
half covered in mud
its bones poking through peeling flesh.
Skeletal fingers grasped the air.
When we gently pulled it from its bed
the arm came away completely.
It had been severed from its torso.
We found that ten steps away
half buried among mangroves
the gnawed remains of a good Christian
whose carcass now sheltered small crabs.
Estrada collapsed in a sob
for he knew the man by the buttons
of a tattered jerkin caught twisted in his ribs.
He was a cook on the Santa Domingo.
We two allowed him his grief.
In truth we felt no better ourselves

when we found six Christians beneath a tree
two with their heads severed.
Estrada threw himself onto the bank
so loud in his grieving
he scared the birds from their branches.
I sat and pulled him close
burying his face in my shoulder
in case other ears than ours heard his pain.

Dusk was falling as we completed our task
of scraping graves and committing
our fellow explorers' remains to Godly burial.
Tears accompanied our labour, but not mine.
For while Castillo joined Estrada
in bewailing our wretched state to heaven
my heart remained dry—I was numb.
I have seen sufficient in my days
to know our life is brutal and short.
I have fought in battles
in which God-fearing Christians sent
each other to heaven with more savage glee
than is seemly among the civilised.
I have witnessed law court judgments
in which a froth of denunciations had
the innocent dispatched before the delinquent.
I have heard sermons so rancid with censure
I swear holy icons turned away in their niches.
Yet still it took me unawares
when in this time of wrought solemnity
Castillo transformed his pain into prayer
and required us to join him in kneeling.

"Lord, we offer up these souls
to Your loving care
which is greater than ever
our poor lives can repay."

I looked at Estrada.
His eyes were tight shut
his knuckles white in twined clasping.
Castillo's eye were wide open
fervently directed at the heavens
as he continued his plea
on our weakened behalf.

> "Yet pure evil has been acted here
> rank savagery in a heathen land
> against good Christians.
> Lord, when Egypt's Pharaoh
> would kill Moses and his tribe
> You rained famines and plagues.
> When Sodom laughed at Your Word
> You removed it from the Earth
> and sent its evil-doers to Hell.
> You rightly reward sin
> with deserved destruction.
> We plead You do so now— "

This was a prayer I could not kneel to.
I remained on my knees
out of respect to those we had buried.
But in my heart I stood and walked away.
I have no issue when men lament
to God their paltry life as men.
I do object when man would play God
and rain Godly judgment on his fellows.
I accept man is often less than man.
Yet I will not call God's wrath onto any
no matter if they have become beasts.
Judgement is God's business. Not man's.

Ө Ө Ө

To my shame in writing these words now
I recall how anger surged through me.
I blame myself for what followed.
So caught up was I in my wrath
I failed to heed what I now suddenly heard:
the nearby birds had ceased singing.
Uneasily, I cast around.
It took what felt an age for my eyes
to adjust to the dusk darkened jungle
and observe what stuck from the shadows:
the head of a spear.
The man holding that spear
surely observed my gaze
for he stepped from the trees.
Five others joined him.
I called in a low voice to Castillo.
He fell silent.
The startled Estrada moaned then stood.
I reached out to hold him
but he brushed off my hand and ran.
A flash of spear succeeded where I had not.
The blade passed through his chest.
Estrada grunted and swayed
the last lamented moment of his living
then toppled to the ground.
Castillo again began praying:
"Hail Mary, full of grace ..."
I remained kneeling
and watched two Indians dance towards me
their spears thrusting, teasing, daring.
They were painted with blood
or with red clay imitating blood.
In my shock I could not differentiate.
It did not matter: their intent was clear.
I felt the toothed prick of a spearhead
dig the bone of my chest.

Fierce eyes glared into mine.
I glared back—and saw hanging round
the savage's gaunt neck
a necklace of human knuckles.
I know I then wondered in my heart:
was this God's sign for me?
Were the wings of a bird I heard in my ears
at that precise moment
actually the wings of the Angel of Death
come to collect a soul
that had tempted its expiration
one occasion too many?
There was no more fight in me.
I flung back my arms
welcoming the death that was mine
since the day of my birth.
With fearless intent
I stared deep into the eyes of the Indian
the Angel of Death had surely stepped into.
The spear's point dug into my chest.
The eyes of my end burned into mine.
Then my head exploded
and the world went black.

4 Cannibals Near Kill Us

OVER THE YEARS I have shaped a surmise:
our sorrow is not our own.
By this I mean sorrow gathers in the hearts
of the angelic hierarchy dwelling above
as they observe the misery
our living makes of our days.
And when their sorrow becomes
too much for even their capacious hearts
it overflows its angelic restraints
and falls from the highest heaven
into this grisled world below.
Here it enters the hearts of those
sufficiently softened to absorb
the sprinklings of celestial sorrow.
This is why our sorrow is not ours
but is given us as a borrowing
that we might share of the life felt by angels.
I further surmise that sorrow
being divine contains distance.
I state this because our act of living
brings us face to face with misfortune
such that at times we do lament our fates
and bewail our wretchedness.
Sorrow is not this self-focused woe.
We sorrow only when the pressing throb
of our present pain recedes
and we stand back from our anguish
to witness how life equally injures all.
This act of distancing opens our hearts
and allows the high compassion
that resides at the very inward of our sorrow

to flower in our hearts
that we might feel for our suffering fellows
that same solicitude angels feel for us—
albeit in diminished human form.
This is why without that angelic sorrow
which showers us from above
all we would feel is misery for our weak selves
and never the divine sentiment of compassion.
This is the glorious gift that enables us
to stand aside from our own paltry pains
and sorrow equally for all.

Perhaps this is too fanciful a conceit.
Yet I had much time to fashion it
over the two days Castillo and I
lay on the ground with arms bound
starved of water and food
while our captors debated our demise.
The problem we faced was cannibals.
Not those who would eat us
but those who had already eaten.
From grunts and gestures
we understood a Spanish ship had foundered
some distance south of the river mouth.
This was surely the San Domingo.
With their food drowned and soon starving
the wrecked made a savage choice:
they began eating one another.
When Indians found the last alive
he was near death and lying among
the gnawed bones of his companions.
The Indians were appalled.
They made great theatre to Castillo and me
that they would never eat their own
even in their most dire hunger.
Only Devils would do that.

And Devils had no place in their land.
So they killed the surviving Christian.
And when they found our companions
who had made their way by oar up river
from the very same San Domingo
fearing an infestation of Devils
they massacred them as well.
It seems tales of cannibalism
were but a Christian-born fantasy.
And what we fantasise too much of
finally impregnates our actions
and we too terribly give it life.

Θ Θ Θ

Castillo and I lay prone
cramped of limb, cracked of lip.
The Indians feared us as devils
emerged from the smoking gates of Hell.
Yet they hesitated to kill us. Why so?
Writhing helpless in the dirt
perhaps we were too emaciated
to convince as flesh-devouring evil.
And Castillo had them intrigued.
Three times a day he struggled to his knees
had me echo his actions
and offered up prayers to our Father.
On each occasion the savages would gather
to hear the words they could not comprehend
but that were clearly reverent in tone.
They were especially mesmerised by
the final four-fold movement of our heads
replacing the gestures
we could not make with hands bound.
During day children would waggle their heads
in excited imitation of our actions.

After our third dawn prayer
a woman brought us water.
That so simple a substance
should prove such a blessed delight!
But when she placed roasted roots
in the dirt before us
a red-painted warrior pushed her aside
and stamped the food into the dust.
I recognised the eyes that glared into mine.
It was a clear challenge.
I learned then how far a man's humanity
depends on his circumstance.
Castillo would have nuzzled
the squashed root like a famished dog.
I commanded him lift his head.
As his eyes queried mine
I knew what he was thinking.
We had prayed for food
and here was the food
God had surely provided.
I shook my head.
We were not the playthings of circumstance.
The warrior watched us with a smile.
With his dirt blackened foot
he nudged the crushed clump of cooked root
towards the wavering Castillo.
But we were neither Devils nor dogs.
They would feed as men
or they would not feed us at all.

The feeding came that afternoon.
A man we thought at first was chief
his face was so gnarled with authority
brought two men carrying baskets.
He ordered we be untied
and with his own hands

gave us drink and food.
He watched with bright eyes
shining with humane intelligence
as Castillo spoke grace
before we, as men, slowly ate.
But this feeding was also a testing.
And he had his own care for our presence.
While we ate appreciatively
I examined the face of the supposed chief
whose expression was one of curiosity
mixed with open good humour.
He had no attack to make.
He was observing and waiting.
What he awaited in due course arrived.

In the failing light of the afternoon sun
our bellies enjoyed a rare repletion.
We then took the opportunity to walk.
Soon our rescuer signaled us to sit.
As the birds' raucous evening screeches
echoed through the jungle
a strange sight emerged from the leaves.
It was a line of weeping savages
carrying a prone boy on a blanket.
The boy was deathly white.
He was gently placed before our rescuer
who removed leaves from the boy's ankle
and revealed blackened swelling.
Our rescuer showed himself a medicine man.
He cut open the wound
cleaning the infection first
by squeezing out black bile and pus
then sucking out the last with his mouth
which he spat into the fire.
From a bag he drew dried leaves
that he wet with a white potion

and applied to the wound as a poultice.
By this time he was working by torch light.
For his last act he stood and danced
circling the prone boy as he chanted
shaking a rattle over him.
He then halted and pointed at Castillo
signalling him to approach.
Castillo did so among the dancing shadows.
He was perplexed.
The medicine man's hand gestures
made clear what they all wanted:
Castillo to kneel and pray.
Castillo glanced at me, puzzled.
I nodded.
They had fed and given us water.
It was right we should give water to them.
So Castillo prayed over the boy.
He finished by standing
and making the sign of the cross.
Uncertain what else was required
he stood still and waited.
For a long time
none made any movement or sound.
We heard the incessant buzz of night insects
the crackling of wood in the fire.
At last the medicine man nodded
and the boy was carried away.
Castillo and I were shown to a hut
and left alone to sleep.
As men. Not dogs.
Next morning we woke to shouts.
When we emerged
we saw the boy was upright.
He was supported by a stick, but standing.
Castillo was offered breakfast
with the reverence due a medicine man.

θ θ θ

Through all the years that followed
I gradually came to understand
the medicine man's gift to us:
our very lives.
He well understood that without
a change in Indian attitude
(given they saw us as devilled men)
we would have died in a day.
He knew also he would cure the boy.
He used the intrigue Castillo's prayers
had already stimulated in the savages
so when the boy escaped death's grip
reverence due the medicine man
was transferred through him to us
and our lives regained legitimacy.
Our survival proved a blessing and a curse.
A blessing for Castillo
who left that morning with the medicine man
as a performing part of his entourage.
A curse for me who was sold into slavery
and lived as close to death
as any man ever experienced.
Such was my fate for three broken years.

5 My Captivity Begins

THE FIRST HOURS I left the village
laid the pattern for what followed.
Two spear-carrying warriors
struck me to indicate the path
as I was marched for seven long days
up craggy mountain tracks
across a plain where grasses cut
the skin on my sea-softened legs
and into a tight-trunked forest
where brambles and thorns
ripped flesh from my face and arms.
I broke the path my guards followed
so they suffered none of my jagged agony.
I could not tell what purpose this served.
Was it to bring me to subjection?
Or did they delight in my suffering?
Certainly they bound me each night
to ensure I could not escape.
And they fed me but once a day
while they ate with audible relish
whenever they desired from rolled leaves
they carried in shoulder-slung sacks.
Yet I determined not to break.

θ θ θ

On the eighth day we reached a river.
Not as wide as that first
I had walked with my now lost companions
we followed its banks for half a day
until we reached a ramshackle village.

My entry was a public beating
among dilapidated mud brick huts
watched by curious children
and yawning men
who regarded me with indifferent eyes.
I was then thrown among the women
whose task was to pull roots
from the river's muddy waters.
I was to find among all the Indian tribes
women carried the heaviest load of labour
helped by fumbling old men
some with bodies too broken to work
whose efforts were despised of all.
Meanwhile the mature men
hunted when hunger hit them
but more often drank fermented juices
danced frenziedly all night
and fought each other at any time
over real and imagined slights
or perhaps merely to relieve boredom.
When exhausted they sat and demanded
they be entertained and fed.
There was no surprise in this.
I had seen the same in Spain
in squalid mountain villages
where the men wasted their lives
and glaze-eyed women
worked until their bodies stiffened
and their muffled nightly weeping
dried to slack-jawed resignation.

Misery is never shy to share its largesse.
It took but one day of servitude
for misery to harrow into me.
The roots of savoured water plants
proved difficult to extract.

After hours of relentlessly pulling
the gnarled plants from sucking mud
my fingers were an agony.
I wrapped them first in grasses
then in fabric torn from my remnant clothes.
They were past being soothed.
And when the pain was too great
and I stood with heaving chest in the water
my guard took up a branch
to beat my head, shoulders and arms.
At least that pain distracted
from my excruciating fingers.
Each night I was thrown roasted roots
I scarce could eat thinking on their cropping.

So passed my first week of captivity.
I was lower than their women
less even than the skin-ribbed dogs
that skulked beyond the shelters
and stole food from the fringes of the fires.
Whoever passed me could demand
I collect firewood, carry water, dig holes
or heave new stones for cooking.
My luck was the season soon turned
and the roots became hard and bitter.
The harvesting halted
and my agony in the water ceased.
Within a handful of days
we shifted to a new camp in stony fields
where prickly pears were ripening.
Two months we remained there
eating the sweet fruit
and drying those that were in excess.
By degrees my fingers healed.
As I learned the savage's routines
and as my presence became common

the beatings diminished
and I at least could walk without pain.
Then Death visited.

Ө Ө Ө

During the wrought course of my years
I witnessed more death harshly dealt
than any would rightly think their due.
With but a skinny twenty-two years
on my well-armoured frame
(and much less a man
than I then thought myself to be)
I fought in the Spanish army
defending the Italian city of Ravenna
against the all-devouring French.
Under the banner of General Pedro Navarro
I was an inconsequential horseman
in a force of two thousand
and another ten thousand pikemen.
The French numbered the same.
It was a battle fought by two Christian armies
equally seeking power and provenance
in the name of religious righteousness
and true service of our all-loving God.
Too young to think any ill of that
I gloried in my presence
among the young fervoured soldiers
whose quick laughter and chested claims
reflected our certainty not just of victory
but of performing high deeds
we would spend the rest of our days
laid up in delirious fire-side recounting.
So we were profoundly confused
when the French began their attack
with two hours of cannon bombardment.

We faced the enemy horsemen
while French artillery stood on our flanks
and blasted us past endurance.
We were commanded to hold
as the earth exploded around us.
The close-packed pikemen behind
anyway made retreat impossible.
Of the four hundred horses and riders
in serried ranks directly around me
fully half were destroyed in those two hours.
Of course our cannon blasted the French pikes.
I thought we might feel the better for it.
Such is the folly of youth.

When the shot was done we engaged.
Spears and pikes, swords and daggers.
Then bare hands and teeth.
All morning and into the afternoon
under the blazing sun
the two forces heaved back and forth
across the slopes outside the walls of Ravenna.
Twice I lost my horse to pike thrusts.
Each time I recovered another from those
that milled on the fringes of battle
too confused by blood, smoke and noise
to make from the field to safety.
I scarce remember much
that followed the bombardment
but I can still see the grass slick
with blood and intestines
and smell the air acrid with smoke
amid the harrowed shrieks of the dying.
All the while our watching commanders
urged us on to ever more butchery.
The young think themselves immortal.
I had sneered with my companions

the night before battle
at the brittle fear-filled talk of those
we thought privileged to have fought before.
That day I learned to fear.
Finally the call to retreat was blown.
As the clouded sky glowed red
from a hill overlooking the field
I witnessed French horsemen
galloping back and forth
using their steeds' hooves to crush life
from those of our spent forces yet breathing.
French pikemen followed
finishing off the writhing few
then ferretting the corpses for valuables:
tunics, swords, boots, coins.
Some cut the fingers of the dead
to collect bejewelled rings.
I do not condemn the French alone in this.
I witnessed Spaniards do the same.
It was on the 11th day of April
in the year of our Lord 1512
during the lost battle for Ravenna
that the chimeras of my youth shattered
and I, Cabeza de Vaca, became a man.

The result of this my initiation
into the chivalries of manliness
was that when I considered the savages
my destiny had cast me among
and when I contemplated their misfortune
in not being born among Europe's civilised
I was not inclined to harsh judgement.
If their women laboured, so did Spain's.
If they feared strangers, everyone does.
If I was beaten randomly, I was their slave.
Yet what next I witnessed well exceeded

even the diminished expectations
life's unrelenting lessons had taught me.

Θ Θ Θ

I woke that morning to weeping.
It was a keening howl
the sort that forms deep in the stomach
and rises in an explosive rush
making a shriek that can sustain for hours.
I emerged from my shelter to witness
a young woman writhing in the dirt
clutching the lifeless body of her son.
Eyes rolled back in her head
howling like a wounded animal
she was in an ecstasy of agony.
One by one others joined her
until the very air heaved
with their yapping and yowling.
Yet one person's pain is another's relief.
Normally at this hour
as the sun's first rays touched the trees
I would be shoved and cuffed
into the start of my long day's labour.
Instead, I was ignored.
So I sat and observed the general lament.

Today I see lament as a shield
we erect around us to hold out truth.
For while we are centred in our grief
the heart-felt coping we must use
to grapple with our loved ones being lost
is delayed until we are sufficiently strong
to accept the finality death brings.
Thus do we hold life's last truth at bay.
Yet the reality before me soon rippled

with an unexpected accusation.
Witchcraft.
One villager had woken from a dream
in which she witnessed an old crone
bewitching the now dead child.
A gnarled finger pointed her out.
I have myself witnessed accusations
made with less substance in Christian courts.
So I was not surprised to see
two men pull a screaming elderly woman
from those huddled round the grieving mother
and drag her through the dust
into the forest behind the village.
I write now I was not surprised.
Yet when the old woman first shrieked
my heart contracted.
Imagining can be worse than witnessing.
I moved to stand and do I knew not what
except a foot kicked me down again.
As the old woman screamed
a furious savage beat me for impudence.
And I shrank within.
What is worse than knowing what is to come
and being unable to act on that knowledge?
The crone's silence ended my resistance.
Then the dogs began howling.
Did they smell human blood?
Or did they too sense the presence
that had freshly ripped
two souls from our fleshly midst?
As the Angel of Death's nails racked
a pained swathe across my troubled heart
my own tortured weeping began.

ϴ ϴ ϴ

From my present perspective
I see my helplessness as key.
Suffering had been our companion
ever since we were shipwrecked in this land.
Folly compounded misery
as superior decisions led us to destruction.
The boats we built to escape
foundered in storms and sank.
More men died as the rafts we constructed
were lost at sea or disintegrated.
Yet in all this we could act.
It was not the world that wholly ruled us
but we made choices and initiated deeds
that swept us towards our end.
But in this malicious village
where a crone was gratuitously murdered
to appease a mother of her child's demise
I was reduced from man to witness.
I was helpless.
Impotence then fed the unexpected:
tears that burst forth
in such an explosion of grieving
that even my captors stared and wondered.

I wept for the innocent crone
who had been cruelly and arbitrarily killed.
I wept for the death of Estrada
another of this world's innocents
who could not learn the lessons of life
sufficiently quickly to survive.
I wept for my several hundred companions
who had sought the freedom of a future
and found only the shuttings of death.
I wept for the wrought world that is
unrelentingly and unchangeably what it is.
And I wept for myself that I was here.

Perhaps I wept most for myself.
For what is any man's particular life
but a God-given occasion
to discover the practice of living
and make that practice an art?
And what is death but a reminder
that we are yet far from what we would be?
Our hopes and dreams
on which we wish to fly
are too often irons that bind our legs
and tumble us into calamity.
Our loftiest desires routinely lead us
to our lowliest errors.
Such, then, was my grievous realisation.
And when at last the pain diminished
and when at last my sobbing stopped
and when at last my hot tears dried
I fell into an anxious sleep
during which the dreams arrived.
Dreams that seared my heart
and tore apart my deepest spirit.

6   The Devouring Web

I ENTERED a domain of dreams.
Night and day devoured each other.
I was devoured.
My waking and sleeping hours met
to become a delirium of despair
wherein past ghosts merged with present
and my famished frame
drooped into the habits of captivity.
Despite my own natural vigour
by degrees I lost that impetus
my life had possessed until those days
through even the travails of shipwreck.
I ended in a sweating fever
vomiting, unable to stand
awaiting the Dark Angel's arrival.
But my pen walks ahead of my story.
I must look back
to tell what occurred next.

θ θ θ

I was born in the year 1490
into a noble family which boasted
little status and less wealth.
In the century preceding my birth
the Christian armies of the reconquista
expelled the Moors from the cities of Spain
until only the caliphate of Grenada remained.
Martín Alhaja, my mother's ancestor
played a crucial role when he placed
the dried skull of a cow

at the mouth of a hidden pass
showing the path whereby Spanish forces
might attack the massed Moors' rear.
The enemy was routed and the King
granted Martín Alhaja a yearly stipend
and in remembrance the honorific *Vaca*.
By my birth the stipend had long dried
and the de Vaca family was shrunk
to serving wealthy nobility as retainers.
For myself I was ambitious.
I used all opportunity to read
in those libraries I was granted access
or prevailed in talking my way into
my goal being to prove myself a scholar
and enter a great university:
Salamanca, Córdoba, Toledo, Cádiz.
That knowledge would then prefer me
to high office in the King's royal court.
Alas, my hopes and my life's course diverged.
I attended no university
and instead served a succession of dukes
in whose minor offices my talents
were squandered on writing letters
and keeping tedious accounts.
By the grand age of twenty years
knowing I would wither if I continued so
I offered myself into the Spanish army.
My aim was to break with my folded present
and wing towards fresh horizons.
Thus it was that in the year 1512
I entered the fields of Ravenna
and there learned what indelible deeds
unfettered ambition leads to.

Doubtful prospects faced me
when I made my reduced return to Spain.

I found service in a variety of courts
where I turned my scholar's mind
into a study of human nature.
I found much to trouble me.
There was the pettiness that ruled lives
in which tongues spoke snaked words
that bent with the designs of the day
to gain a perilous finger-hold
in the rough climb to office and privilege.
Four years I diligently and loyally worked
in one duke's stifling employ
in order to achieve a coveted role.
But I lacked the ruthlessness required.
Lies removed me from the race.
When I heard the sniggers follow me
as I walked the castle's devious halls
I observed this truth:
once a questionable deed is done
the perpetrators must convince all
righteous justice was really performed.
Hence they fortify their action by fencing it
with ramparts of justifications.
If any then dare question their motives
or point to those they dealt with unjustly
they turn round their joint artillery
and blast those who would stand to them.
Watchers always adopt the winners' stance.
Thus does fear make men cowards
and injustice boldly perpetrate its intent.
With the gaggle of manipulators
now bound by their shared perfidy
their only course is to speak more boldly
of their personal integrity, position, power
and denounce those dissenters
who dared speak them as they are.
I found the higher the office

the lower those who occupied it.
Some urged me to wield the same weapons
to obtain what to my talents was but due.
I chose to find service elsewhere.
But even worse was at work.

Behind the bright tapestries commissioned
to celebrate Spain's victory over the Moors
a darker intent underwove her celebrations.
With the Moorish presence extinguished
and to confirm now all Spain as Christian
it was time to expel the Jews.
In the years following my birth
the Royal Decree of Alhambra forced Jews
to either convert to Christianity
or leave Spain forever.
To uproot your family from a town
your ancestors occupied for centuries
and move to a foreign country
where strangers are viewed with suspicion
is no easily achieved task.
Naturally many converted to Christianity.
In truth, some among these converso families
had been Christian for three centuries
and were proved well loyal to duke and King.
This was no longer sufficient.
The dark machinery of the Inquisition
was let loose in Spain's cities and towns
where it peered into converso hearts
and pulled from them evidence
they lived a devious doubled existence.
What happens in a land
where duplicity must be rooted out
yet the very accusation itself
may be uttered duplicitously?
Suspicion thrives and devisings soon decay

the rank-tilled ground of civil commerce.
With so many to suspect
a misheard whisper was sufficient
to bring the Inquisition's gloved fist
pounding the door any hour of night or day.
So why in the troubled year of 1520
did I marry Maria Marmolejo
a woman of Jewish descendent
whose family had converted
to Christianity but thirty years before
and whose face clearly bespoke her lineage?

It was not an action I deliberated long.
The Marmolejo family were tailors.
I needed a new suit of clothes.
I found Maria's father Pedro Marmolejo
deferential in the way of tailors
yet his conversation was urbane.
I gained more than new clothing that day.
In due course I met Maria.
There are occasions when instant accord
brings us close to another
due to a feeling that as human beings
we are walking in the same direction
or have drunk from the same well.
Maria was well-educated and sultry
and wore her knowledge of the world's ways
with nonchalance and ease.
I was smitten.
After due civil process we married.
And for the first year in my life I was happy.
We both were happy.
Then the Inquisition's gloved knuckle
pummeled the Marmolejo door.
And the happiness fell out of my world.
Some claim a year of happiness is more

than one lifetime may rightfully expect.
I ask how Pedro Marmolejo could be
thirty years an unquestioned convert
yet it was suddenly necessary
to test his fidelity to our religion and King
by peeling his flesh in the torture chamber?
Of course, it was not necessary.
The torture proved nothing
but that when you bend a man he cries.
Yet having flung the accusation
those who pointed at him could not back away.
The one prevailing truth of the Inquisition
was that accusation always led to judgement.
And judgement to the faggots.
Pedro was strangled before he was burnt.
I was instructed to be grateful
at the granting of that small mercy.
The fire that climaxed Pedro Marmolejo's life
seared deep into my own vexed heart.
Yet what occurred next was worse.
I castigate myself still for my error.

Maria had been born Christian.
She was baptised and confirmed
in the rituals of the Holy Catholic Church.
So she was beyond the Inquisition.
Yet Medina Sidonia was a small town.
I should have taken her away.
But I was born there
and my family was well-regarded.
I thought it safe to remain.
I arrived in our rooms one evening
to her palpable absence.
A small case of her belongings was gone.
I never saw or heard of her again.
In desolate times I yet fear the worst.

Slave ships frequented the southern coast
and all knew children and women
were snatched off streets or from markets
to disappear into ships' bilges
and be conveyed to the slave markets
of Tangier, Tunis, Algiers, Alexandria.
Or perhaps Maria was encouraged to leave
by Christians who disapproved her staying
but promised safe passage past the city walls.
How much I needed to believe that.
My long-standing enchantment
with the city of my birth expired.
I vowed then but one place
would satisfy my desire to escape
the mercy of my fellow Christians:
the New World and its free environs.
I shall not extend on the ironies
lurking within that assumption.

ΘΘΘ

Civilisation is a veneer.
Yet are we but savages at heart?
In the long months that followed
the innocent crone's pointless death
I went deep inside myself.
Each day I laboured for my captors
collecting, carrying, cutting
suffering the stings of captivity
as I was cuffed, kicked and beaten
while toiling deep in forests and clearings
forgotten and lost in an uncaring land.
And at night I was visited by dreams.
At first it was as if I entered catacombs
where the musty dead still lived
decaying in their stone coffins.

I shuffled in memory's mausoleum
reviving this misunderstanding
remembering that omission
recalling that blunder
errors of judgement
slights received and given
until the stacks of my sins swallowed me.
Then the dead awoke
and I was caught in a maelstrom
of regret-filled memories
so wrought and full of emotion
that each dawn I emerged from sleep
hollow-eyed and inwardly mangled.
What were my memories?
My failing Maria pierced me
near past all enduring.
I had been too involved in my position
as secretary to the King's cousin
to observe changed attitudes around me.
Once the horrors of Pedro Marmolejo's
trial and execution were past
I convinced myself it was over.
My view was fabricated of hope woven
of one part denial and two parts delusion.
We each possess times we regret
when we are so wound up in certainty
we do not see what was there
when we walk a dubious path
turn to find the door slammed shut
and discover there is no returning.
The truth is I was warned.
One afternoon in the duke's study
he hinted there were plots in train.
I chose to think he spoke of another.
One dusk I saw men lurking near the rooms
I shared with my beloved Maria.

I saw them as another's dawning terror.
Darkness roared over me
when Maria vanished forever
and I perceived I had lied to myself.
It was a lie born of hope and fear
yet a lie nonetheless.
There is no going back from errors
of that magnitude and consequence.
I sought to escape them by leaving Spain.
Thus I joined an expedition to Florida
led by Governor Pánfilo de Narváez.
But I could not escape myself.

ϴ ϴ ϴ

As my numbered months of captivity grew
again and again I woke at dawn
or deep in the corrosive night
burning in the fires of remembered dreams
that embedded me in a past
it seemed I would never evade.
I was as a fly entangled in a web
of my own wrought fabrication.
Each night I lay trembling in its threads
reliving the terrors I myself
had conjured in the course of the travails
that I brought on myself and those I loved.
The web's strands were woven of fire.
I burned in their purgatorial grip
till my very heart cracked open
and all I thought I was
everything I had built myself to be
showed itself as petty and deficient.
In those fires I was reduced to the state
of Job in the wilderness.
I lack the will to conjure a full image

of what I experienced those burning nights
or the griefs that wracked me each waking day.
Hence I shall make no attempt
to tame them now through the stylings of art.
This ends my account of that tortured time.

7 From Hope to Despair

THUS PASSED two years of captivity.
My clothing, the accoutrements
of Old World refinement, those symbols
of my superiority to my human fellows
all shredded, wore off, rotted away.
I ended naked as a new-born child.
In the eyes of the New World's savages
ignorant as they were of Spanish civilisation
perhaps I had always been a naked man
and I merely now perceived myself as did they.
Naturally this New World
was not the new heaven and new earth
long promised by the prophet.
Yet I was renewed in it.
Emptied of pretence and pride
Cabeza de Vaca was now
what he had always been
except education and ambition
had caked and veneered his outward visage.
Truly, Cabeza de Vaca had become
a nullity looked down on by all.
So it was I resigned myself to my fate.
Or at least attempted to do so.
Yet fate was far from done with me.

ɵ ɵ ɵ

One dawn I woke from a new dream
in which a Spaniard called to me.
He was in a familiar forest
among trees where now I worked.

Three days after I saw him in the flesh.
A tribe from the coast had journeyed there
to gather walnuts from a grove
women from my tribe also harvested.
For a time a skirmish promised
as warriors on all sides of the clearing
notched arrows and shaped with spears.
But none had the heart to fight.
And when each tribe's women
broke ranks and crossed to greet and hug
all weapons were lowered.
They spent the afternoon carousing.
I of course was commanded to pick walnuts.
There I discovered
also gathering walnuts in the dappled sunlight
a scrawny naked Spaniard.
He was the man of my dream.
He was equally startled to see me.
We observed our captors ignored us
so edged together and conversed.
His name was Lope de Oviedo.
In part I knew him already.

Ɵ Ɵ Ɵ

Following the loss of our five ships
on the storm-ridden Florida coast
we had no choice but to trek
through the untrammeled forests
in search of hospitable land and treasure
to claim for our Emperor Charles the Fifth.
With some hundreds of men
and but four horses and miscellaneous stores
trekking proved an imposing task.
For three days we met no one
and our provisions declined alarmingly.

At last we found a small village
of but a dozen poor Indians
with whom we exchanged trinkets
for their stores of corn.
Here Governor Narváez heard tales
of the magnificent city of Apalache.
The Indians gave wide-eyed descriptions
of storerooms overflowing
with provisions of all kinds:
corn, fruit, nuts, exquisitely woven blankets
and soft suits made of deer hides.
Especially wondrous to them
was the gold Apalache had cached
from years of triumphant trading.
The Governor was impatient for success.
Apalache promised the sensation
he required to sustain his governorship
while the gold would serve to requite
those in Spain who had invested
in our journey of imperial expansion.
Therefore he led three hundred men
myself and Lope de Oviedo included
into the forests in search of Apalache.
Captain Dorantes commanded the remainder
whose allotted task was to scavenge stores
from our wrecked vessels
and establish a safe and provisioned base.

Apalache was a disaster.
When we finally found the fabled city
it proved to be a ragged forest village
of no more than forty families.
There was no gold.
There was scarcely sufficient corn
to feed those of us who reached there alive.
We remained in Apalache twenty-five days

searching the surrounding territory.
We found a gold necklace
and two blankets wafted with gold thread.
Nothing golden else.
We also suffered continual attack
by savages who quarrelled when we stripped
their villages of that little they possessed.
They rushed us before dawn
slayed a Christian or two
then dissolved back into the darkness.
When the Governor admitted finally
we had been misled
our weakening force took four weeks
to fight back to Dorantes on the coast.
Our men there were equally diminished
through sickness, starvation and Indian assault.
Neither did the scavenged stores
we hoped would feed our strength
prove sufficient to provision us for long.
The truth was we needed to escape that place
before all sickened, starved and died.
Our only hope was to build boats
by which to sail from the catastrophe.
We used what suitable wood we could find
to make five vessels sufficiently large
to each carry fifty men.
Melted buttons and buckles made nails
while from clothing we shaped sails.

In adversity you come to know a man.
Throughout our ordeals
Lope de Oviedo impressed me.
As second in command I was the ear
for those complaints none would dare voice
directly to our imperious high Governor.
Not once did Oviedo complain.

He marched stoically on our jungle slog
from Apalache to the coast
and used sound judgement in a swamp
when two horses slid deep in mud
and so panicked that one horse drowned
all the while Indians flitted beyond reach
flying poisoned arrows to further prick us.
Oviedo's stoicism under duress
earned him much gratitude that day.

Ө Ө Ө

Oviedo whispered to me in that walnut grove
providing news of our fellow Christians.
I had heard nothing of Andrés Dorantes
or the three he had taken inland
all those many confused months before.
Neither did I know Castillo's condition.
Oviedo's news was that
all surviving Christians were captives.
The medicine man had traded Castillo
for blankets and dried herbs.
He now worked with women
in a village three days to the south.
Diego Dorantes and Figuero were enslaved
in a village two days inland.
Both Estevanico and Oviedo himself
were living on a large island
a day's travel from the walnut grove.
Two other Christians were captive
on other parts of the same island.
Three more were the slaves of a chief
who headed four forest villages.
Andrés Dorantes was the freest.
His prowess in combat
had so earned him Indian respect

that he accompanied war parties
and joined attacks on rival tribes.
A wounding had swelled his name
permitting him to travel alone.
Thus he met all the Christians
surviving in the surrounding territory.
Travel had equally enabled him
to reconnoiter the country.
From this he had formulated a plan.
Come the first full moon of spring
Dorantes proposed that all we Christians
should escape our captors
and meet on the coast
directly opposite that large island
where Oviedo and three others resided.
Dorantes would provide a canoe
for them to make their escape.
All would then march together north
maintaining safety in numbers
until we either met Christians
or Indians who would lead us to them.
How much a man can bear
when a plan provides a future!
I had but five moons
before we would gather our resources
and march from captivity.
How little do we truly know.

Ө Ө Ө

That cold and desolate winter
impatience sore tested me.
I had never before so seen in myself
those throbs of balled energy
that sought to burst their bodily bounds
and stamp my will on the world.

This I observed in myself
through long inert days sat dully in a hut
filled with the empty ache of hunger
watching the rain batter
the village's dirt yards to mud.
How much I raged within
at the fate that held me there!
How urgently I wished I already walked
with Dorantes and my fellow Christians
from this exile among the ignorant!
Yet those throbs of impatience
formed the links in a new chain
that bound me ever more tightly
to the captivity I so craved to escape.
For impatience infected me with rage.
And rage festered into resentment.
And resentment reared as carelessness
that crushed all my hopes.

It was but fourteen days before
our strategised meeting on the coast.
I was collecting firewood
from the forest late one afternoon
when a drunk young buck
began cuffing me as I carted branches
up an incline behind the village.
He claimed I was too slow.
I knew he was displaying his prowess
before those laughing striplings
with whom he had been drinking.
But all day I had been considering
the injustice of my captivity
and was a fevered ball of rage.
On being struck
rage caused me to throw the branches
under whose weight I staggered

directly towards my assailant's chest.
I was too weak for such rebellion
and they landed in a clatter at his feet.
The striplings' laughter died.
They first looked at me wide-eyed
then turned towards my attacker.
He immediately hoisted a branch
and rained on me such a flurry of blows
I was driven back towards the incline.
I balanced a moment on its lip
as wood broke on my head.
I then lost my footing and fell.
His bent honour straightened
he spat at me as I lay twisted
among fallen and rotted trunks
walking away in a squall of laughter.
Yet my troubles were but beginning.
The fall that saved me from further attack
had lanced a snapped branch into my back.
When I moved pain speared through me.
I rested panting a while
knowing none would come to my aid.
My situation was simple:
either I helped myself or I died.

I gritted my teeth and braced myself
then hauled my body off the branch.
I used leaves to staunch the bleeding
and pressed them in place with binding bark.
Then I began the slow climb
up the slippery incline.
It took till nightfall.
I waited in the undergrowth
until all entered their huts to sleep.
I then went to the dying fire
and used the glowing wood ends

to cauterise the wound.
I collapsed in exhaustion and pain.
For three weeks thereafter
I drifted in and out of delirium.
The world and my dreams became one.
An old woman tried to feed me
except I vomited her food across a mountain
I had climbed during my childhood in Spain.
I felt myself again on our ship
as we battled the winds off Florida.
And I watched Andrés Dorantes
standing over me as I lay flat on the deck
dripping with the spume of raging seas.
I lived all over again past errors and sins
that had so hurt myself and others.
And I felt the Angel of Death's soft wings
brush my pulsing heart
while I quivered in the dismal realm
between the living and the lived.

Ɵ Ɵ Ɵ

When at last I returned to myself
and had strength to stand
I emerged from the hut
and witnessed an empty village.
The tribe had transported
to their seasonal feeding grounds.
My imminent death was anticipated
so I had been abandoned.
Only an old woman was left
to wring water from a wet cloth
onto my fever-cracked lips.
When my death at last occurred
her task was to roll my body
into a pre-dug hole in the ground

and cover it over.
Looking at the sky that night
I observed the moon was past full.
In my impatience to be gone
I had missed the planned escape!
The woman told me what transpired.
Andrés Dorantes and his brother
visited and witnessed my sickness.
They believed with the Indians
that I indeed would soon die.
They left the bow and quiver of arrows
intended to purchase my freedom
to pay for my care until I died.
The old woman was that care.
On hearing this tale I swear
my heart contracted within.
I did not know what I least preferred:
surviving the fires of fever
or burning to death in its embrace.

8 Tasting With Butterflies

NO MATTER the power of our strength
at times we must put vanity aside
and draw on others' kindness to survive.
I may have over-leapt my expected death
but I remained too weak to walk ten steps
let alone follow Dorantes and our men
on an extended jungle trek.
My present urgent task was recovery.
Nursed by the able Indian grandmother
for whose ministrations I am ever grateful
I did those same tasks I performed in captivity:
hauling water, collecting firewood
gathering berries, stoking the fire.
Yet I did so now in freedom.
In part that freedom lay in lack of coercion.
But more it was my bubbling impatience
and my accusing resentments
had all but boiled away.
During the course of my burning dreams
and the debilitating fever
the last civilised veneer that riveted my life
had fallen from me.
I was now suspended in a still state
neither seeking to escape
nor not seeking it
neither happy nor unhappy
and certainly no more shackled by the cares
that had brought me to the edge of death.
So passed a full month of recuperation.
Alone with my nurse in that empty village
night after night I sat in glowing firelight.

And with that peace came a deep perception
that I shall attempt to project here.

Θ Θ Θ

The smells come out at night.
As the humid heat of the sweating day dies
and the raucous evening chorus fades
the night jungle begins its darkened song
and rich scents float above the clamour.
The clicks and scratchings of insects
the high croaks of frogs
the deep-throated howling of monkeys
the haunting hoots of unseen fowl
the slithering undergrowth
where sudden shrieks break out
then as abruptly fall silent again—
this is the pulsing soil
from which rise the smells of life and death.
I well remember the odour of damp earth
borne on the breeze from distant plains
that told of life beyond the hedge of trees.
I recall the viscous perfume of night flowers
a thick sticky sweetness
that drifted above the dank wetness
of decaying leaves and rotting plants.
And the musk of a prowling cat
a thin waft of death
that silently slipped through the jungle
then paused to stare with black eyes
from behind a screen of braided branches.
These smells conveyed what is
sensed but ever remains unseen:
the night jungle's mystery and terror
its paralysing danger and intoxicating delight.
Immersed in the thick thrum

sung by the rain forest's vaulting life
I was transported out of myself
into a world beyond the human.
I heard the delicate stepping of ants
climbing between spikes on cactus stalks
towards the giant white discs of flowers
that opened only to the cool night air.
I saw tiny staring dragonfly eyes
hovering above the shimmering surface
of a moonlit pool
then watched the flash of their wings
as they darted across a wash of glassy water
touched by blushing streaks of dawn.
I felt the sleek skin of the lizard
as it scurried over heated rocks
its sun-glinted back pricked
by a high gliding hawk's hungering gaze
and savoured the cool embrace of earth
as it slithered into the safety of its burrow.
I tasted with the trembling butterfly
the balls of yellow pollen
it lifted on its snaking sticky tongue
from the narrow throats of flowers
and was intoxicated with it
by the blazing carpet of swollen blossoms
across which it flitted and swooned.

Did it take near dying to appreciate
the dazzling rapture of being alive?
We men share this crawling mewling space
that quivers between Heaven and Earth
with a world of enthralled creatures.
Yet caged within our hemisphere of swagger
whether walking the hot streets of Spain
or fawning in a jewelled lord's fevered halls
attired in the cut cloth of our self-regard

we too eagerly buckle our ambition and
chain our selves into a circumscribed life.
What I learned those long jungle nights
is the art of setting aside
my human desires and projections—
to be still and allow the living world
to send out its subtle tendrils
and slowly, by silent degrees
infiltrate the deep fissures of my heart.
Only then do we penetrate the surface skin
of this Earth's teeming abundance
and learn what God has with such tender care
so deeply and delicately embedded in it.
Only then do we hear the world's secret whisper
and learn the devastating lesson
of what a petty imperious thing is man.
Those days of my recovery from death
provided among the greatest insights of my life.
And I further see now
as I pen these words in my cramped study
that all my catalogue of travails
each unwanted pain I pulled myself through
did but tenderise me in readiness
for a vision of all the things that are
in their wholeness of being so.
Yet I perceived this truth only in part.
The fullness of an engulfing worldly vision
yet awaited in my future.
I had first to negotiate my present.

Ɵ Ɵ Ɵ

I woke one morning to discover
the old woman, my nurse, had departed.
There are occasions in life when
our future course shifts abruptly

a new path is revealed
and a decision must be made.
Would I stay? Or would I leave?
Choice required confronting my fears.
Was I so yoked to the certainty of servitude
so fearful of singly facing the jungle's dangers
that I would stay and wait my captors' return?
Or would I step into the dark unknown
of my own unforeseeable future
and risk again being a plaything of death?
My father always claimed of me
that I was too much an impatient lion
that I needed to lie with the lambs.
Yet it is one thing to imitate our Saviour
and become a lamb before God.
It is another to be so tethered by our fears
that we stake ourselves to our present
and proffer our passive self
to the blade and barbecue of others.
I took a blanket hide, roasted corn
a small gourd of water
and set out for I knew not where.
Given voracious death prowled the forest
and the difficulty even of finding food
I knew this might be my last day of living
on this marvellous yet uncertain Earth.
But I stepped out with no regrets.

9   I Am Saved by Shells

WHAT WAS IT I had now become?
Naked as a savage yet I was not one.
I had the heart of a Spanish Christian
yet heard no sermons
nor did I bend before any altar—
unless those wilds be counted my church
my heart had become that church's altar
and my life's trial was God's sermon to me.
I had passed through the purgatorial fires
of my own deed-devised anguish
and emerged purged of my previous self.
The child baptised Cabeza de Vaca
had in this New World been born anew.
As who? Into what? I cannot say.
The very act of naming the human soul
asks more of words than they can yield.
On the paradox of creaturehood
theologians have spent reservoirs of ink.
And since they cannot decrypt the riddle
of intertwined spirit and blood-surged body
I would advance no claim
to know what makes us as we are.
What I do know is in walking from that village
I was no longer civilised.
Yet nor had I become savage.
I was both more and less than what I was.
It was that simple. And that complex.
Larger minds than mine are needed
to plumb the deeps of that mystery.

ǝ ǝ ǝ

The days following my village departure
were a stumbling of surprises.
I slipped—and fell into a berry bush
where I lushly appeased my gnawing hunger.
I was paused one noon
savouring the noisy hot riot of nature
the radiant flowers and arguing birds
yet with an empty gourd
and uncertain of my direction.
I then heard faint trickling.
Pursuing the sound I found not just water
but a fish flopping on the stream's bank.
I dared sleep only short spells for fear
my carcass would tempt prowling beasts
yet I survived in a hungry land
where creature feeds on creature
and man has no exceptional status
that removes him from the daily bill of fare.
Some would say God guided my feet
bestowing care from harm.
Yet how much was it divine providence
how much my native cunning
and how much mere stumbling luck?
I cannot in conscience say
God opened a safe path just for me.
But neither are my powers so robust
that I was my sole cause of resilience.
This is yet another mystery
I add to all those that puzzle heart and mind.

I ended one warm day on the ocean's edge
cooling my feet in the surging waves.
Looking down the curve of whitened beach
that vanished into a haze of swirled sand
I perceived myself in paradise.
Such is the joy of leaving what we know

to discover what we can scarce imagine.
I lay later under trees
replete from eating fat oysters
I found clinging to tide-sucked rocks.
I had no plot or plan.
I well remember my thoughtless head
as I watched the flushed clouds fade.
I then stretched onto my back
and marvelled at the jet-black sky
studded with a wash of winking stars.
I felt so elated that night
I allowed myself to drift into sleep.
I woke next morning with knowledge
of how to negotiate my survival:
I would become a trader of shells.
So simply stated it sounds a whimsy.
But I had witnessed women with necks
decorated by strung rows of tiny beads.
And I had seen hand-sized shells used
to cut food and scrape meat from skin
and to slice a bean-like plant
that when fermented fuelled festive dancing.
Inland tribes hungered for these shells
trading hides and arrow head flint
which in turn were sought by coastal tribes.
I foresaw I could deliver a bounty to each
while travelling freely across the land.
So in practice it proved to be.
Humble shells transformed my life.

Θ Θ Θ

Since our inopportune wrecking
mine had been a cramped existence
controlled by those who saw no more in me
than a beast to be burdened

by that same drudgery they abhorred.
I now experienced greater freedom
than ever Spain afforded me.
The irony was my freedom resulted
from the restrictions warring provoked.
The land was divided into tribal territories.
None could traverse another's terrain
without risk of violent riposte.
Thus little trade occurred.
My weakness now became my strength.
Being affiliated of no tribe
I easily slipped between boundaries.
And being but one weaponless man
I presented no threat to any.
Rather I conveyed those luxuries
that smoothed the rough in their savage lives
and added sweetness to their travails.
As word spread of my goods
each village entry became a warm welcome
and a safe spending of the night.
I soon was receiving orders
for hides used in ceremonial costumes
decorative tassels woven from deer hair
red ochre to dye hair and paint faces
stiff cane and flints for making arrows
and glue and grass twine for binding.
My trading territory was large.
I travelled far towards the inland mountains
and some fifty leagues up and down the coast.
I grew familiar with the country.
I mentally mapped river fords and passes
and beheld the safest paths and most dangerous.
There was much to celebrate in all this.
Yet I suffered privations and ate only
when those I traded with had food.
When they did not we starved together.

I watched a half day once
from a ledge high on a valley slope
as a hunting party of six braves pursued a deer
they so confused with their circling
it ran in diminished spirals.
When exhaustion at last led it to lay down
they caught it with their bare hands.
Those were times of largesse
when an entire village feasted and danced.
At others the village fasted.
Yet whether replete or starving
they maintained their exuberant joyfulness.
I walked once with a tribe
so famished they were reduced
to eating lizards and flying insects
worms, serpents and ant eggs.
Some I saw devour spiders.
When I asked why they endured this state
which seasonal planning would overcome
they laughed and said it was not long
before the prickly pears ripened
and their now shrunk bellies would stretch.
Yet their hopes then remained skeletal
for fruit ripening was many moons away.
When I said so they shrugged.
Thus their spirits waxed without waning.

Θ Θ Θ

Winters were the worst.
Cold cracked the lungs.
Frosts were so sharp they cut the feet.
I remember losing my way
in fog one bitter morning and stumbling
into a swamp where I near drowned.
Shivering and lost, I walked some time

seeking the path I had missed
when I sensed a presence behind me.
I turned of a sudden
and witnessed a tawny cat with flicking tail
staring at me from a distance of ten steps.
I several times shouted to scare it.
It blinked back at me.
I charged with waving arms
and it quietly stepped into the jungle.
With all haste I shaped a spear from a branch.
That cat stalked me for hours.
Eventually I spotted a small cave on a rise
in front of which I piled wood.
Yet my hands so shook
I scarce could strike the flints to make flame.
With hard rock at my back
fire at my front and spear in hand
I waked through the longest night of my life.
Next dawn I praised God for my survival.
And when at last the fog lifted
I discovered I was but two hundred steps
from the village I sought.
From then I followed the Indian course
and spent the winter weeks under cover.
Yet these years proved fascinating
as my trade enabled me to observe
in all their intimacy the fascinating customs
diverse tribes chose to live and die by.
Such customs I shall briefly now describe.

10 A Miscellany of Customs

TO BEGIN this brief account of customs
I shall state what must by now be clear:
the New World state of dress was undress.
However, some women wore loose cloaks
woven of moss scraped from trees
or deer hides if the wives of medicine men.
Among men was a wide-spread practice
of piercing their nipples from side to side
and threading through the hole a thick reed.
Some by this same means pierced their nose.
Yet many tribes lacked piercings altogether.
The lesson I learned of this
is the degree to which our identity
is grounded in social agreement and custom.
Thus are we shaped by our place of birth
and what we wear and how we deport ourselves
results less from who but where we are.
Such, at least, is my observation.

θ θ θ

Drunkenness is ubiquitous.
Some smoke herbs on festive days
prepared by local medicine men
who each keeps his ingredients secret.
For the rest is a liquid
prepared of leaves plucked from the water oak
a tree that grows in clumps on swamp edges.
The leaves are roasted in closed clay pots
to which water is twice added and boiled off.
The hot foaming liquid is then drunk

in a constant cycle of brewing and sipping
until the men are too stupefied to walk.
From this pastime women are excluded.
Indeed should a woman approach the men
during the preparation process
she is beaten and all the liquid discarded
for fear evil spirits would enter their cups
and capitulate them to early death.

ϴ ϴ ϴ

Women have the harshest life.
In the years I laboured beside them
I heard of all their weariness and pain.
No man deigns to carry the burdens
piled on women and the captured enslaved.
While some village huts are permanent
all tribes perambulate in a seasonal cycle
trekking from fruit groves to seafood beds
to forest edges where deer graze.
They live in small lodges with woven coverings
and shaved branches for poles.
Easily folded and carried
it is women and slaves who shoulder the task
when travelling from one ground to the next.
I witnessed in many tribes
when the season came to crop roots
the women spend the day in digging
and the night stoking fires
that make the roasted roots palatable.
They slept but four hours a day
and were beaten if exhaustion made them slow.
And through all this they still
prepared food and cared for the tribe's children.
Then when bleeding each month
they were driven from the tribal circle

to eat alone of food none else would touch.
Such is the poverty of women's lives
in a scant land commanded by unbending men.

Θ Θ Θ

Though I never witnessed formal marriage
men do take wives.
However should a man not enjoy his wife
or should she prove too much a scold
he is free to discard her for another.
But once children are born
a man and his wife are locked as one.
Children are much loved by all
and suckled until ten or twelve years.
This is entirely practical
for all tribes periodically lack food
and children are too tender to thrive.
Yet one tribe I visited flagrantly violated
this common course of care.
Ever fearful of surrounding enemies
they would not have their women marry
outside the tribe and give birth to braves
who could grow to subdue and enslave them.
Yet neither would they marry their women
to relatives or their own tribal men
from a fear such shared pedigree is evil.
Therefore each unneeded new-born girl
was thrown outside to be eaten by dogs.
When those tribes' men wished to wive
they purchased a woman from their enemies
for the cost of a bow and two arrows
or a fishing net one fathom square.
Thus they shaped their happiness.
Young married men suffered many restrictions.
Whatever hunted game they caught

custom required they pass it to their wife
who took it to her own parents' home.
There her mother cooked it
and her father decided what food be returned
to the young buck and his daughter.
In this way the young men were kept in check
and the tribe ensured its women
were at least sufficiently well treated
to labour for the good of all.
Then there was the intoxication of war.

θ θ θ

Warring provided universal recreation.
I never witnessed such cunning
as the devices each tribe employed
against their ranked enemies.
Their prowess would convince in Italy
where continuous battling
has honed the skills of Spain's finest.
When tribesmen feared enemy attack
they positioned their lodges
on the very edge of dense forest
or backing onto swamp
so there was but one available approach.
They then opened an indistinct path
into the thick jungle and made a sleeping patch
to keep safe their women and children.
Next the braves dug trenches
near the lodges where they would sleep
of enough depth to hide a man.
The trench was overlaid with brushwood.
They were so well hidden by this contrivance
that even when standing directly overhead
they remained invisible to the eye.
Yet secreted loopholes allowed them

to observe and even fire arrows.
At dusk they lit fires they refreshed all night
to confuse any spying enemy.
If any were then sufficiently foolish to attack
they leapt from their hiding places
and loosed such a flurry of arrows
that in one swift swoop
their assailants were surprised and devastated.
I once was with a tribe named Aguenes
on a moonless night
when their guard was relaxed
and they were surprised by the Quevenes.
With lodges burning and arrows flying
the Aguenes fled into the forest.
After the attacking Quevenes had departed
the Aguenes emerged to number their losses.
Three had died. Others were cut and bleeding.
The braves collected the spent arrows
then tracked their assailants to their own village.
At dawn they attacked with such ferocity
that five Quevenes were killed
and almost all the others wounded.
It took the arrival of both tribes' women
to cross the violent divide
and calm the men's reciprocal fury.

Θ Θ Θ

One remarkable custom I witnessed
between the Cavoques and Han.
The tradition is that when two tribesmen meet
they sit half an hour weeping before speaking.
When the requisite time is passed
they then happily exchange news
as if neither had so wept.
And when their meeting is complete

the visitor is given by the host
all that he has to hand
which the sighing visitor takes away.
Indeed I witnessed once an exchange
in which two wept near an hour
then the visitor departed
with gifts of heart-felt friendship—
all without a word being spoken.

θ θ θ

Much else powerfully struck me
during my years of trading shells.
I shall describe them as they illuminate
this account of my New World adventures.
Yet word of Christians I ever sought
as I journeyed from village to village.
What had happened to Dorantes
and his group of escaped captives?
How many were they? Where were they?
Did any other Christians yet live?
I heard confused descriptions
of a Christian living in this village
or drowned in that swamp.
Yet when I sought out those places
the story proved an exaggeration
or a fantasy told to enthuse me
because my trading goods were craved.
Other tales were tangled memories
of strangers tagged to some other time.
The truth was that in the Indian memory
one month, one year and one lifetime
were all balled together into a single past.
It meant tales were rolled out at will
for whimsy, diversion, and to entertain.
I travelled and asked and witnessed.

But the news I sought remained scant.
Until the day at last arrived whereby
I gained so very much more than I sought.

[87]

11 Escape Is Delayed

IT WAS WHEN I began my third year
as a successful trader of shells
that I decided I required a new plan.
I well remember standing
on the lip of a well-grassed plain
watching the sun lower over the mountains
as I reviewed what I had discovered.
I had explored the region's coast
and found no sign of Dorantes
nor any members of his band of escapers.
Neither had I discovered evidence
of new Christian arrival and occupation.
The truth of our plight was clear.
No recovery expedition sought us.
We were shipwrecked and alone.
I thence decided I had but one option:
to traverse the mountain range
that towered hugely before me
and cross it to the Pacific coast
where Christian presence was certain.
Of course the way was doubtful
and the coast so distant
endeavour might reveal it unreachable.
Still the journey beckoned.
I had only stride into the setting sun
and embrace the conditions of my fate.

Yet life is never so simple.
For while I felt driven to keep walking
neither could I leave behind Christians
the King had commanded to my care

who for all I knew yet survived.
I well understood my hopes were hollow.
Did any other Christian truly live
in this land of savagery and starvation?
My ignorance made me helpless.
Yet I had no choice but to fulfil my duty
as a Spaniard, a Christian and a man.
So while trekking towards the Pacific coast
was my one saving course of action
I decided to delay its execution.
Thus I turned from the mountains
and began the twelve day tramp to the coast
in a final attempt to discover
if any of my companions yet survived.

Θ Θ Θ

Newfound zeal is the most determined
and so the most rewarded.
It brought me to Lope de Oviedo.
I had crossed the water by canoe
to trade ochre and flint for dried food
with Indians living on a large island.
And of course to seek Christians.
I found Oviedo standing on the beach.
Discovering that we each lived
amazed and punctured us both.
He thought me long dead
and I thought him to have fled
with Andrés Dorantes and his men.
We exchanged both tears
and word of the past years.
I told of my survival and he of his choice.
Fearful of retribution by those tribes
whose territories they would transgress
he had declined Dorantes' escape

and reconciled himself to a life of safety
with the Cavques Indians
who he named even-handed and kindly.
As to the fortunes of our companions since
reports of Christians had reached him
from tribes who fished the inward sea
between island and mainland.
Yet whether any Christians were alive or dead
Oviedo could not confirm.
My estimation was he feared all word.
For if our companions had escaped
he would lament his decision to remain.
But if they had died on their escape
then he would be alone in the wilderness.
Knowledge would bring either regret or pain.
He avoided both by choosing ignorance.
Such is one way man copes
with the burden of being man.

I stayed a month on the island.
My urgent goal was to persuade Oviedo
to search with me for our compatriots.
But he was caught in a web of obstinacy
born of the fear that suffocates risk.
I feared I should soon depart alone.
Then we heard significant news.
An island tribesman brought word
from a mainland trading expedition
that five Christians lived with local tribes.
Furthermore he had seen a black man.
This was surely Estevanico.
That moment our emotions soared
and Oviedo's opposition melted.
When I now repeated my plea
that we seek out our shattered remainder
he happily agreed we should do so.

I thought this an excellent sign
that our fortunes were turning.
I was soon reminded how little I knew.

Θ Θ Θ

In the boats of island Indians
we navigated the waters to land.
We left tribal women foraging for oysters
and progressed south along the coast.
Presently men I well knew from my trading
emerged from the jungle.
They knew nothing of Christians
but we walked a pleasant while together.
Yet when we reached an inlet problems began.
Our companions met six young braves
from a tribe named Deaguanes.
At first the meeting proved fortuitous
for while they knew nothing of a black man
they had news that two Christians
lived in a village but two days away.
From their descriptions it was clear
these were Dorantes and Castillo.
And the tribe holding our captains
would soon be visiting a close by walnut grove.
But we heard bad news too.
Men of another tribe held two more Christians
the soldiers Esquivel and Mendez.
Some in the tribe had dreamed a terror
had killed their kinsman
and decided our countrymen were that terror.
They were killed for it two moons ago.
This remembrance so excited the Deaguanes
that they adopted the bullying bravado
I witnessed of innumerable young warriors
in Europe equally with the savages here.

Thus they held Oviedo and me to the ground
and pushed arrowheads to our throats
threatening they would finish us
the way their cousins had our countrymen.
In this was much self-preening and laughter.
I saw it as but boasting show
and that forbearance would weary their play.
But Oviedo was not so composed.
When my Indian friends intervened
by distracting our tormentors with food
he sat shaking under a tree far longer
than two minutes of jeered taunts justified.
His unease was multiplied soon after
when the six braves returned
and cuffed and kicked Oviedo
to show they could complete their threats
whenever they desired.
And I was not excepted from their care
receiving my share of their attention.
After the braves had departed
and we each gingerly addressed our bruises
Oviedo proclaimed his mind was changed.
He had decided to return to the island's safety.
I protested that our true safety was together.
But he was resolute.
He heartily embraced and thanked me
for the good cheer I had brought him.
Then he turned and walked away.
I sadly watched his solitary trek
to rejoin the tribeswomen we earlier left
collecting shellfish up the coast.
My deep sorrow was that at the very first test
Oviedo so readily proved a waverer.
I comforted myself by thinking
that after I found Dorantes and Castillo
and planned with them our flight to safety

I would return for Oviedo.
I little knew it would become
another added to my list of life regrets.

θ θ θ

The Indians spoke truly.
I found Dorantes in a walnut grove
just two days' after Oviedo departed.
On seeing me he went rigid
all colour drained from his beaten face.
When he recovered his poise
he proclaimed he had thought me a ghost
so certain he was that I had died.
Such was the general report of me
despite my circuitous travels in trade.
Having persuaded him I was flesh
I desired to learn of our companions.
He then recounted all that occurred to him
after he left me dying of fever.

That time almost three years before
Dorantes had gathered thirteen men
this being the full number he found yet living.
Their names were Alonso del Castillo
Andrés and his brother Diego
Esquivel, Benitez, Tostado, Chaves
Valdivieso, Austuriano the priest
Huelva, Mendéz and Estevanico the Berber.
Francisco de Léon was found
on the second day of trekking.
They journeyed north for eight days
avoiding all Indian contact
concealing themselves in the jungle
whenever they heard people or smelt fires.
Thus they cautiously explored the coast.

Dorantes' hope was that other Christians
had survived the years of travail
and together they would form an enlarged force
that offered security of numbers.
But they found neither Christians
nor signs that any still lived.
Fourteen mouths soon depleted their food.
Hunger and uncertainty then bled
the momentum from their expedition.
Forced to forage
they inevitably met tribespeople
Dorantes had been at pains to avoid.
There was at first amity among them
as the savages happily shared their food
with the famished Christians.
But after a time a savage stood
and took hold of Chaves by the arm
to lead him away to his village.
Huelva and Esquival caught Chaves' other arm
and resisted the savage's impertinence.
Suddenly the air bristled with spears.
A scuffle ensued followed by a chase
in which Dorantes led the Christians to safety
by plunging into a swamp.
However Francisco de Leon saw snakes
swimming in the rancid waters
and fear kept him quivering on the shore.
A warrior's arrow ended his indecision.
Satisfied the insult to them had been repaid
the savages jeered at the Christians
covered in weed and swimming with reptiles
then turned their backs and departed.
Francisco de Leon died very soon after
coughing blood in Dorantes' arms.
Thereafter the group lost purpose.
Dejected, they argued much that night.

Next day half trekked back south.
Not wishing to return to captivity
Dorantes led the remainder inland
where they stayed with friendly Indians
in exchange for their labour.
This agreement lasted a full year.
It ended one storm-blown night when
ten savages attacked Valdivieso, de Huelva
and Andrés Dorantes' own brother Diego.
The savages killed them for no reason
but their own drunken fun.

Next day the savages were a choir of remorse.
But after Dorantes had buried the three
he led Castillo, Chaves and Estevanico
back south to rejoin their companions.
Over the two years following
the Christian numbers slowly diminished.
The deaths of Esquival and Mendez
I have already recounted.
Chaves died of drinking bad water.
The priest one day led Estrada and Tostado
out into the jungle to pray
And they were never seen again.
Huelva joined Oviedo on the island
where he died of a snake bite.
Valdivieso became melancholy
and refused to work
no matter how the Indians beat him.
He died half of starvation
and half eaten within by worms of despair.
Of our original five hundred empire builders
only five now remained alive:
Dorantes, Castillo, Estevanico
Lope de Oviedo on the island
and myself who rose from the dead.

θ θ θ

Two days after meeting Dorantes
I was reunited with Castillo and Estevanico.
It was near five years since our broken raft
had brought us starved to the golden sands
and savages saved us with roasted grubs.
In the midst of walnut trees
with hot streaks of sunlight falling across us
we hugged each other in a delirium of joy.
We then knelt and Castillo spoke a prayer
thanking the Lord for His good care of us
through our exquisite trials.
As we sat and spoke our Spanish tongue
all past wretchedness was dispelled.
It was the happiest day
we each had lived in this unforgiving land.

I wasted no time in proposing my plan
to traverse the countryside and reach
our fellow Christians on the Pacific coast.
As a project it dared nature, man and fate.
Yet Dorantes, Castillo and Estevanico
ardently embraced it as our only hope.
Each saw we must act to save ourselves
else savage caprice would finally kill us
if New World jungle and fever did not.
Yet we could not depart on the morrow
for those tribesmen whose slaves they were
had grown dependent on their toil
and would surely track us if we vanished.
Our best opportunity to escape
was during the annual harvest of prickly pears
when many tribes gathered to feast
and trade arrows, bows and skins.
Our strategy was to arrive with the tribesmen

and depart with an inland tribe
after devising some reason we must do so.
Yet we had a full six months still to wait
before the autumn season of prickly pears.
In that time we could proffer no clues
for if the tribesmen learned of our plan
they surely would kill me
so not to lose their valuable slaves.
But neither could I depart now
and return closer to the time of leaving
as unforeseeable accidents and incidents
each day threatened to alter our lives.
None knew what could and would occur
over the six months yet to come.
Hence I decided to remain.
I gave myself in labour to the Marianes
with whom Dorantes had taken shelter.
Castillo and Estevanico toiled as slaves
for the neighbouring Yguaces tribe.
Thus we sought to survive as one.

θ θ θ

The salting of our soul is a curious process.
One man runs from what another pursues.
What one thinks opportune
another sees as threatening his life.
Truly, what we conceive is what we see
a projection from what we desire to be so
onto the tapestry of our worldly exploits.
How else explain the difference in views
one man to the next?
Oviedo sought safety in that same world
I viewed as lacking safety.
I sought to escape what he embraced.
I observe this as a prelude to our next trial.

Lope de Oviedo died that summer.
He and a tribesman were fishing from rocks
when a giant wave swept them out to sea.
Seven days after the Indian's body was found
battered and half eaten by fish.
Oviedo's body was never recovered.
Word reached us a full month later.
I know Oviedo had his fate.
He willingly embraced the choices he made.
Yet still I regret I was not more forceful
in bringing him to the bosom of our care.
Yet disaster also generates strength.
The shock of Oviedo's sudden death
made us yet more determined to escape.

12 Fields of Spikes

PRICKLY PEARS are a difficult fruit.
        Egg-sized and red or purple in colour
covered with tiny unforgiving spikes
they bloom on cacti in autumn.
We four captives trekked four days
with the Mariannes and Yguaces tribes
through jungle and across grasslands
arriving one cooling afternoon
as the sun lanced long shadows
across the dry and stony fields.
The cacti stood above a man's height
in green clumps that grew beyond sight.
The tribes stayed two months of each year
feasting on the ripened fruit
and drying excess for the lean winter months.
After a season of roasted roots and nuts
the pear's juicy melon taste relieved the palate.
However it carried a sting in its skin.
The cacti's long spikes were easily snapped.
But the fruit's skin projected tiny hair-like spines
that penetrated unprotected fingers
and caused discomfort that soon built to pain.
These spines were removed by gentle burning
or rolling the pears in dirt.
They could then safely be peeled and eaten.

Within an hour of our arrival
the first of the season's fires were lit
and the task of gathering fruit begun.
We were in the early season
but easily found sufficient pears for eating.

We knew from past visits
that our labour would be confined
to picking and de-spining fruit
with occasional forays to collect water.
As the tribesmen relaxed
our beatings diminished to nothing.
Within the week six tribes more arrived
and our Indians were wholly occupied
in feasting, making music and dancing
interspersed with brewing sharp tasting liquor
they fermented from cactus juice.
This was both welcome and convenient
for we four each carried cuts and lesions
we required time to heal ourselves of
in preparation for stepping out on a trek
I anticipated could well endure a year.
But what of my companions fate had enjoined
to embark on such a doubtful adventure?
Each had his own history.

Ө Ө Ө

First was Captain Andrés Dorantes.
Born in Bejar, a village near Madrid
he was of modest strength and size
but carried himself with composure and poise.
Weaponry, navigation, construction
knowledge of plants and herbs
and an ability to read men's hearts
coupled to pragmatic decision-making
made him a formidable enemy or friend.
He was shipwrecked on the Azores once
and kept ten sailors from starving
while avoiding discovery by Dutch raiders.
Not one man had died when he at last attracted
the saving attention of a Spanish galleon

nigh on six weeks after their wrecking .
Of our entire company of six hundred
he was the one man I expected
to surmount any difficulty.
I had ensured he captained my vessel
when we left Cuba for Florida.
I backed him now to sustain our survival.

Second was Alonso del Castillo Maldonada.
Etiquette demands he should have precedence
over the lesser rankings of Dorantes and myself
but such concerns have long fallen from me.
Truth to tell I never warmed to Castillo.
Native to the cathedral city of Salamanca
son of a doctor and duke's daughter
his lack of practical acumen or skills
meant he often failed his captain's duties.
Yet pride meant he would never admit
he was less than his position required.
When circumstance exposed his incapacity
he became a bully who demanded fealty
from the competent he commanded
which created resentment in his men.
A devout Christian of somewhat noble birth
he recoiled on those occasions
he felt our fathers' faith was being crossed.
His creed then dragged on our powers.
Yet as my account will shortly make clear
he carried a special blessing of our Lord
that proved crucial to our safety and escape.

The Moroccan Berber Estevanico
was the powerful third of our party.
An Arab Negro from the city of Azamor
which the Portuguese plundered in 1513
he was among those captured and enslaved.

A large man, physically commanding
yet quiet and deferential
he proved a naturally talented sailor.
Dorantes observed his skill working the sheets
and purchased him during that voyage.
Through all the many years since
Estevanico had been less Dorantes's slave
and more his trusted deputy.
After our wrecking on these shores
Estevanico's size and blackness
detached him in the tribesmen's thoughts
from we smaller lighter-skinned Spaniards.
He also quickly learned Indian tongues.
All this meant he suffered fewer beatings
than did the rest of us
yet did each day's toil without complaint.
He thereby earned respect from the savages.
That respect I afforded him also.

The fourth was Alvar Núñez Cabeza de Vaca.
My pride is astuteness and tenacity.
I sought never to complain at adversity
nor to gloat over success.
I ever hoped to wear command lightly
as had my grandfather Pedro de Vera
conqueror of the Grand Canary Island
for the great glory of the Spanish crown.
From him I drew the spirit of adventure
which carried me so far across the Empire.
I believe men found me upright in dealing
if at times too principled for worldly advance.
Yet I never took anything of another
nor came to judgement without evidence.
I have sought always to carry myself
dutifully before man and God
and ever to sustain just and honest actions.

Yet I never professed to be more than I am.
The good Lord alone knows if I succeeded.
Such was the odd band of survivors
God selected from our original six hundred
to complete an unanticipated task
the possibility of which we doubted
even as its scope unfolded before us.
That task began within the week
among the fields of spikes.

Ө Ө Ө

Early one crisp autumn dawn
as our tribesmen slept off their drink
three desperate Indians sought us out.
They claimed they had for three days
suffered aches in their stomachs and limbs.
Their tribe's medicine man was absent
so they demanded we perform a cure.
The reason they determined we could do so
was because one was present years before
when the old medicine man
had saved Castillo and myself from death
by cannily encouraging Castillo
to pronounce a prayer over the sick boy
who recovered that very night.
Our visitors sought that saving prayer now.
At first Castillo refused.
He feared retribution if he failed
and foresaw failure as a certain outcome
given the medicine man's skill
and not his prayers
had saved the dying boy all those years ago.
Yet the more Castillo declined
the more enrapt the three became.
At last the men's excited shouts

[103]

woke the slumbering tribesmen.
A circle of fascinated Indians gathered
and it was plain there would be no escape:
either Castillo spoke the prayer
or we were all in danger of reprisal.
To show we jointly shared the consequence
I knelt behind Castillo in prayerful gesture.
Dorantes and Estevanico echoed my action.
His confidence thus bolstered
Castillo commanded the Indians kneel.
He first stood a long while in silence
gathering his meager powers.
He then spoke his prayer:

> "Great Father in Heaven
> we live within Your Mystery.
> We know nothing but that
> You have plans for each and all.
> We know not why life is as it is.
> We know not why these savages
> crave of us the solace
> only Your touch can bring.
> Yet we are Your obedient servants
> and they Your suffering children.
> They beg You now for health.
> Lord, whatever You choose and will
> we are content to love and accept.
> Through Jesus Christ. Amen."

We three echoed that Amen.
Castillo ended making the Sign of the Cross.
All were silent as he remained standing
his upheld arms beseeching the Above.
And we continued kneeling
awaiting whatever consequence came.
It was a moment pregnant with doubt.

Yet in twenty heartbeats an Indian leapt up
and with loud cry shrieked, "I am cured!"
Promptly the two other kneeling Indians
surged to their feet also
and began shouting and dancing.
An enraptured hubbub swelled the air
as the watching Indians joined their fellows
in an ecstatic dance of the restored.
But Castillo merely lowered his arms
and turned to us where we knelt
too stunned by this mystery to speak.
He raised his hands in a gesture
that echoed our own confusion:
what had just transpired here?
But the Indians knew.
They had been cured of dire illness
by that mighty medicine man
the God-powered Alonso del Castillo!

Ɵ Ɵ Ɵ

The cure in the fields of spikes
both exhilarated and perplexed us.
Exhilarated because it was no failure
and we would suffer no negative consequence.
Perplexed because it was no failure
yet we knew not what it was.
Were the Indians mistaken?
Perhaps it was in their mind they felt ill
so it was in their minds they were cured?
This meant God lifted not their illness
but rather a veil in their heads.
Or had they lifted it themselves?
Perhaps they were lying outright
for some reason only they comprehended?
Which meant Castillo had done nothing at all

and their illness and cure was theatre and show.
Whatever the truth of this so-named cure
two sequels hard followed the morning's events.
First the three Indians brought us all they had
in gratitude for their miraculous healing.
If this was only theatre and show
they were playing their roles to the utmost.
We were caught then in the quandary
of deciding how to dispose the gifts.
Castillo contended whatever had been done
was wholly the reach of God's power.
We could not accept a gift that was God's.
However Dorantes said we must accept
for such was the custom in these lands.
Not to do so was perceived an insult
and insult led always to violence.
Castillo responded the custom in Spain
was for the gift to be passed to God's Church.
But there was no Church here to do so.
I proposed a solution: We receive the gifts
use just a small portion ourselves
and pass the remainder to those around us
in the sanctifying name of God.
That way we honoured the givers
and honoured God whose power all is.
This is what we did.

The second sequel occurred next dawn.
We woke to six Indians waiting patiently.
Each carried an ill of some kind
and refused to depart until they were cured.
This caused us further consternation
because we were yet unconvinced
the three Indians had told the truth.
What if there was no healing, just trickery?
Other waking Indians gathered around us

while we debated what our action should be.
We had no choice but to assay a cure.
Those with cuts and contusions
Dorantes and I salved with watered ash.
We then had all bend before Castillo
who solemnly uttered his prayers
while we knelt behind, intoning our Amens.
Would they be healed or no?
Together, savage and Christian, we waited.
Were we more relieved or frightened
when the six leapt to their feet
and danced a celebration of restoration?

Θ Θ Θ

Success intensified our quandary.
We woke now each dawn
to discover a new group of the sickly
waiting their turn to try our healing powers.
Castillo vigorously deflected their attention
telling them not he but God was the healer.
His words failed to convince.
The Indians well understood a superior Power
in the beginning created the world
animated all creatures in it
and so possessed the potency to hurt or heal.
But that Power did not act through all.
We four were the chosen vessel
and they revered us for it.
Castillo privately thought them primitive
for worshipping the branch and not the root.
I never spoke it aloud yet wondered
if they were more religiously attuned than we.
In our heads we carried a mould of rightness
given us by our religious betters
against which we measured the world's events.

Whereas they directly perceived what is
with neither judgement nor presumption
and simply feared or thanked
the perceived Power for what occurred.
Despite our thoughts and feelings
and no matter what the explanation
our lives now bent in a direction
none of us could have ever foretold.
And it presented an opportunity to escape.
As the days shortened we knew
our tribes' time here would soon end.
If ever we would escape it was now.
So one bright midnight
after the evening's drinking was done
and our tribesmen soundly slumbered
we did what proved most simple
and slunk away from our captors.

13 The Burning Tree

WE WALKED from the fields of spikes
the moon's waxed luminance ensuring
we did not stumble where we would stride.
Anxious the tribesmen not track us
we travelled apace through the cacti
hoping the stony ground concealed our steps.
Our relief was palpable when by dusk
there was no evidence we were pursued.
Yet our aloneness was both blessing and curse.
For the autumn evenings had turned sharp
and we required shelter for the night.
As the sun set we spied smoke
and turned our feet towards it.
We soon chanced on an elderly man
who leapt from the bushes on seeing us.
Seeking to allay his fear
we sent Estevanico ahead to assure him
we would wreak him no harm
that indeed we had travelled a great distance
entirely to greet him and his tribesmen.
The stratagem worked.
The old man's fear abated and he agreed
to guide us through the scrub to his village.
He scuttled ahead to announce our arrival.
We soon smelt smoke on the chilled air.
We then met four braves of the Avavares tribe.
Their carriage was welcoming but wary.
They spoke the language of the Marianes
with whom they yearly bartered bows.
We assured them we came in peace
and sought only their kindness and company.

Their response was gratifying
for they happily led us to their homes.
And when word swelled we were those
who had healed in the fields of spikes
a feast of prickly pears was laid before us.
After eating a familiar scene then played out
with ill villagers begging we heal them.
The moment Castillo completed his prayers
and over their heads made the Sign of the Cross
all leaped up and proclaimed themselves cured.
They then brought yet more prickly pears
and slices of venison so numerous
we knew not where to stack them.
That night the entire village celebrated
feasting and dancing till dawn.
When they woke next afternoon
they began their carousing over again.
In all they feasted three days
honouring our presence and practice.

Θ Θ Θ

By the fourth day enough calm prevailed
that we were able to enquire
about the land laid out before us.
We asked how many tribes lived inland
and what kinds of food grew there.
Their response deflated our hopes.
The land was full of prickly pears
but the season was ended
and those tribes which harvested them
had already departed for their winter grounds.
The land contained scant sustenance
and was emptied of people.
Worse, winter here was hard
while the open country afforded no shelter

from cold, wind or storm.
After a single terse discussion
we decided to winter with the Avavares.
They were well content to quarter us.
Indeed our arrival among them was timely
for within two days they too departed
the now depleted fields of prickly pears.
The journey involved four full days trekking
across grasslands that afforded no food.
On the fifth day we reached a river
where the tribesmen pitched their lodges.
This was to be our winter residence.
Dorantes and Estevanico were housed
with the Avavares' medicine man
while Castillo and I dwelt with his son-in-law.

Θ Θ Θ

The cold months we dwelt on that river bank.
Yet no man can occupy another's house
without working towards the mutual good.
Therefore I negotiated a contract
whereby we made them what they needed
and they in exchange fed us.
Thus we turned our hands to fashioning
combs, arrows, bows, nets
and the matting they used for their lodges
all of which needed repair
to make them watertight for winter.
The Avavares men avoided such work
for it kept them from hunting.
A hunt's duration was often two weeks or more
as deer cropped five days' journey away
and several days more were needed
for six men to track and trap sufficient deer
to make their hunt worthwhile.

Our offer to do the work they would not
leaving them free to pursue game
was therefore most readily accepted.
My major lament of all the tribes
was none planted seasonal crops
or properly planned their yearly cycle.
During the course of our travels
I saw fields fit for excellent pasture
and farm land fat with promise
that could well sustain regular cropping.
Yet the tribes preferred a happenstance life
trekking between customary feeding grounds
doing what their fathers did
and their great-great-grandfathers before them.
They shucked oysters or plucked fruit
when the season was high
backed by what game they by chance caught
then happily hungered between seasons.
The Indians were immured
to the rhythms of feast and famine:
none complained when nigh to starving.
We suffered much learning the Indian way.
Yet while we would devise our future
in truth we remained helpless
to whatever it was, whether fate or chance
that placed unforeseen circumstance on our path.
I was to learn that lesson again
in a Job-like hazard that near took my life.

θ θ θ

My trial began one mid-winter dawn.
Storms had kept us shut in for days.
But once the skies had cleared
and the sun weakly warmed our skin
we formed a group of twenty

[112]

and departed the village
to stretch our legs and search for food.
In particular we sought pods that grew
on a tree resembling the bitter vetch.
We soon separated in the straggly woodlands.
For myself I enjoyed the solitude
as it was many months since
that I had rejoined my fellow survivors
and we had been continuously together since.
So I relished these few hours alone
pleasantly reminded of my trading days
when I wandered the wilderness
passing whole weeks without human contact.

The vetch pods proved elusive.
I walked ever further into the woods
yet sighting the sun for orientation.
When the mid-afternoon chill began
I was confident of the direction
to reunite with my companions.
However after travelling a full league
I found no trace of human passage.
Indeed I discovered in a small clearing
a bitter vetch tree with no pods stripped.
I was now in a quandary.
The day's warmth was rapidly waning
and I had no idea which direction to walk.
Many times I called out.
Only the birds answered.
Then my ear caught the sound of water.
I proceeded that way and found a spring.
It quenched my thirst
but not my desire to find my compatriots.
By now it was bordering on dark
and I had to tell myself I was lost
naked and hungry in a pitiless land.

I knew if I did not find shelter
that night I would likely freeze to death.
Helpless, I engaged the one act left to me:
I bent my knees
lifted my face to the heavens
and from the utmost depths of my heart
beseeched the protection of the Lord.
It was a quiet conversation
such as passes between intimates.
I thanked the Lord for His care
and pledged my negligible life
to the preserve of His pitying hand.
If He choose to sever my soul from body
I remained well content
for even in the depths of abject poverty
I had lived a richer life than many
and a deeper life than most.
Whatever came I was prepared.

I know not how long I knelt there
eyes closed and heart open.
By degrees I felt a breeze puff around me.
Carried on the breeze was the scent of smoke.
I concentrated on the smell
to discern the direction from which it blew.
I then stood and walked that way.
My thought was the smoke marked a village
whether of the Avavares or some other tribe.
It proved to be quite otherwise.
I presently entered a wood of blasted trees
where burnt branches hung over my head
such that I did eerily feel
I walked between the seared ribs of Death.
The ground beneath my feet was cloaked in ash
being sharp with stones and blackened thorns.
Presently I spied a faint glow.

In the gloom I carefully advanced towards it.
I soon witnessed a remarkable sight:
a large burning tree
surrounded by blackened trunks and branches.
I approached and was suffused
by invigorating heat.
I fell on my knees and thanked the Lord.
That providential fire was my survival.
How had such an enigma come to be?
As I kneeled with heat on my face
I thought of the burning bush
Moses discovered on the sacred slopes of Sinai
from which spoke the voice of the Lord.
Of course I was never a Moses
and no voice croaked from the crackling wood.
Indeed, I knew the burning most likely
resulted from a storm-blasted lightning strike.
Yet as I knelt and bathed in the burning
by degrees I felt myself transported
to that bliss-filled time which is no time
but transmits the stillness and peace of Heaven.
I know not how long I huddled there
wholly immersed in that inward silence.
But when I returned to myself
pre-dawn light edged the horizon.

Θ Θ Θ

I left the burning tree carrying firewood
and a smouldering brand
such that I could set a new fire when needed.
Two days of walking brought me to a stream.
I decided my best course
was to follow this stream's flow
to whatever river it spilled into
then hew to the river bank.

My hope was at the last it would lead me
back to the Avavares' village lodges.
My survival stratagem was simple.
Each evening before the sun set
I halted wherever was shelter
and with my hands scratched a shallow hole.
I then built four fires surrounding the hole
using firewood I scavenged from nearby trees.
I next made bundles from the long grass
that grew beside the water
blanketing myself with the bound stalks
before laying in the hole to sleep.
By this means I survived each night's chill.
My fortune was no northerlies blew
and no seasonal rains stormed
that regularly drenched that region.
Yet there was an irony in this.
For though well protected from cold
the truth is I near died of heat.
I woke one night from sleep
to find the brush with which I was covered
set alight by drifting sparks
so that my hair was made aflame.
I extinguished it by rolling in the dirt
but my scalp still bears witness to that mishap
in two patches where hair has not grown back.
In all I spent five days and nights
without a mouthful of food
my feet bleeding from the harsh ground.
On the sixth day I met Avavares Indians.
They and my companions were much surprised
thinking me dead of a snakebite
or some other wrought circumstance.
We feasted that night on prickly pears
the taste of which had never been sweeter.
Yet to this day I savour the night

I spent transported beside the burning tree
and tender thanks for my survival
naked and alone in a devouring wilderness
that few men enter willingly
and fewer still safely emerge therefrom.

14 A Buried Arrowhead

TWO DAYS hard following my rescue
we found ourselves besieged of Indians.
Five from a nearby tribe were partly paralysed
and begged of Castillo his healing power.
Among all those sick who had come to us
these were the most hopeless we had yet seen.
Their limbs were palsied
and the feet of three proved so twisted
they were unable to walk
being conveyed by relatives in a litter.
The hands of two were turned inward
such that they were unable to hold a bowl.
And these crooked complained of many aches.
They tendered such an assembly of sorrows
and our hearts so trembled for them
Castillo willingly added his hopes
to those of their weeping bearers.
Yet this was a far from ordinary cure.
Castillo spent a full half day praying
that their afflictions be lifted.
At dusk, exhausted from his efforts
he commended the crippled to God
and we sat in silence to wait what transpired.
The hours slowly passed.
Nothing occurred.
As midnight gripped our bodies
we drifted into sleep amid uneasy doubts.
We woke at dawn to shouts.
Two of the crooked now stood and walked
their bent feet straightened.
Paralysis in the others was much diminished.

The two with twisted hands
broke their night fast by feeding themselves.
The wave of euphoria generated by this cure
rippled not just through the Avavares village
but through the entire tribal region.
Hundreds of the ill from nearby tribes
now sought our therapeutic attention
from among the Caltalchulches and Caoyos
and the more distant Maliacones and Susolas.
Nor do I forget the Atayos tribesmen
who daily exchanged arrows with the Susolas.
Yet when they came in supplication to us
seeking release from their torments
there was no quarrelling or fighting.
Neither would we brook any in our presence.
Indeed, our stipulations were so successful
they often gave us their bows as gifts.
Thus we sought to cure them
not only of the illnesses that ravaged them
but also of their savageries of character.
Whether we succeeded or no
only God and the cured may truly answer.
We did the best we could
within the paltry reach of our powers.
Yet among all the healings that winter
one stands out as most particular
in how it altered my expectation and standing.

Θ Θ Θ

Some days after Castillo's prayerful success
we were approached by Susolas warriors.
One among their revered elders
was much grieved of an ancient hurt
that stood him now on the brink of death.
As the Susolas dared not convey him

to us among the Avavares riverbank lodges
they uttered a heart-felt petition
that Castillo trek to their village
and there practise his powers on one
whose past deeds argued his present preserving.
Castillo's response startled us all.
He was adamant he would not attend.
The problem lay not with the Susolas
but in the confines of his self-doubting mind.
The straightening of the halted and twisted
had disturbed him profoundly.
The Indians hailed the healings as miraculous
and we led them in celebration
of our Lord's great power to do so.
But Castillo quailed in the comparison.
He considered only our Saviour
and His annointed Apostles possessed
the authority and power to perform miracles.
Discord soon swelled in his heart
expanding the gap between his heavenly hopes
and his own perceptions of himself
as a mere man mired in wickedness.
With us all Castillo's hope was for salvation.
Yet his fear was that he harboured such sin
that the good he did in the curings
was undermined by the ill
he felt accompanied his every step.
In truth he feared his obdurate sins
would open a hole of hypocrisy
in the hidden unsayings of his heart
through which he would fall
into the eternal fiery punishment of Hell.
So strongly did this fear envelop him
that he refused to hear the Susolas' pleadings
finally removing himself to his lodge
to prevent their further supplications.

In so doing Castillo created a quandary.
For the Susolas then turned to me
saying I should perform the healing.
The Avavares joined them in their pleading
claiming I was surely as powered by God
as was the well-proven Castillo.
In truth, I had spoken prayers
over the ailing in the fields of spikes.
Yet so had we all during those times
when the waiting ill numbered too many
for Castillo's single ministrations.
The Indians' entreaties were heart-felt
their confidence in me unshakable.
But saying something is so never makes it so.
Words require the substance of proof.
I feared I was insufficiently substantial
to sustain the burden of their expectations.
Yet it was clear one among us must go.
And I was that one the Indians had chosen.
Yet were they the sole arbiters in this matter?
The events that followed were suggestive
of another Hand's involvement.

ϴ ϴ ϴ

Our way to the Susolas village
lay through sodden jungle
and across swollen boiling streams.
Once we climbed a jagged cliff face
supposedly to avoid a hunting party
visible only to Indian eyes.
We suspected them of theatre
to impress on us their prowess.
We also knew the Susolas loved warring.
To ensure my safe return
I left Castillo to the Avavares' care

and with me took Dorantes and Estevanico.
There was a double strategy in this
for we wished to explore inland
and gain more knowledge of the terrain
we planned to traverse come spring.
Our exploration was humbling.
The Susolas' village was a handful of huts
huddled on the banks of a gushing river
in a land without visible food supply.
Yet not the landscape but the ill man
required the first fullness of our attention.

He lay in straw on a hut's dirt floor
eyes glazed over, panting with pain.
I at once doubted any could stop him
soon tasting the bitter fruit of death.
When he began whining in his torment
I feared he would expire before me.
But he presently settled
and drifted into uneasy sleep.
His pain was caused by an arrow head.
Years before, during a tribal skirmish
the arrow had pierced his back.
When he fell the shaft snapped
and the head lodged deep between his ribs.
A fellow warrior's fumbling attempt
failed to draw out the sharp head.
Being far from their village
there was no medicine man to call upon
to tend the buck back to health.
Yet the body has a cunning all its own.
Under a leaf poultice
the angry swelling soon receded.
Both flesh and skin consequently
healed themselves so quickly
the strong buck soon walked unaided.

Decades followed in which he felt
only occasional twinges of pain
mostly in the wet winter months
when damp infiltrates the bones
and probes all ancient complaints.
But of late the arrow head had shifted.
It now lodged agonisingly against his heart.
Thus the Indians' concern.
A dozen crouched in that silent hut
and stared at me with expectant eyes.
I knew myself for no surgeon.
But I had witnessed on the battlefield
what the skilled hand could achieve.
So I administered a soporific
Dorantes had learned to make
from secretive tribal medicine men.
I spoke a prayer over the prone man
and the strangest night of my life began.

What we think we can achieve
is always less than what truly is possible—
provided we first entertain the notion
that the impossible may be achieved.
I deliberately emptied myself of doubt
and prayed a greater Hand
would enter my unpracticed fingers
and do what I alone and unskilled could not.
I then began my work.
With a flame-purified knife blade
I cut open the Indian's breast
carefully slicing through bloody flesh
till I reached the sharp metal.
The arrow's point was caught
in a wedge of thick cartilage
and additionally lay athwart my cut.
Judicious cutting and digging was required

before I was able to start extracting
the cause of the warrior's pain.
The arrowhead was very long
and required infinite patience
to lift it from its bed of tissue.
In that small enclosed hut
surrounded by twelve fetid bodies
sweat slid continuously from my brow
and seeped stinging into my eyes.
Frequent stoppages were required
for Dorantes to mop my face.
I then quickly resumed
fearing the longer surgery lasted
the more likely the warrior would expire.
His good fortune—or sound fate—
was to be breathing when I finally
extracted the offending arrow.
I stitched the gaping wound
using a stout needle made of deer bone.
Promptly I was begged by those present
to make them a gift of the arrow.
I held it up over my head
uttering a brief prayer of gratitude
then ceremoniously handed it over.
Aching and trembling with fatigue
I crawled to the hut's corner
sunk onto a pile of deer skins
and fell into a deep and dreamless sleep.
Such was my inauguration
into the mysteries of surgery
wherein an untutored physician
achieved more than he ever knew to do.

15 We Eat Dog and Depart

OUR CHRISTIAN taste for miracles
is shared with every nation.
Such at least is my observation
made in the fervid aftermath
of my unanticipated surgery.
Just one day after the arrow was removed
I cut the stitches that closed the wound
and discovered healing was complete
leaving but a thin raised scar.
The patient declared he suffered no pain
and boldly wrestled a young brave
to prove to all he was fully cured!
As this warrior was held in high regard
that estimation was transferred to us
and we three were roundly hailed
as miracle-dispensing sons of the Sun God.
All the expectant Indians of nearby tribes
who then flooded into the Sosulas' village
to feel our marvellous healing touch
proved the sincerity of their reverence.

Such was the demand for relief
we sent for Alonso del Castillo
that we together might attend
the superabundance of aches and hurts.
Even the Berber Estevanico
was required to dispense blessings.
Our procedure was simple.
First we prayed over the patient
then blew breath over that part
of the body that was afflicted

this being an Indian practice
that all our implorers desired of us.
Finally we made the sign of the cross
over their bowed heads
and sent them smiling on their way.
We never heard of a case
when those to whom we administered
did not proclaim themselves cured
of whatever pain they came burdened by.
This healing occupied us many days
until we were heartily sick of it.
Our relief was palpable when
the first buds of prickly pears
thrust themselves into the world.
We were decided this was the moment
we would begin our long-planned trek.
But first we must solve a problem.

θ θ θ

All experienced traveller know
a journey demanding endurance
must set out from a bedrock of strength.
Yet we were far from strong.
At issue was diet.
During the hard winter months
those we healed shared what they had.
Yet that proved inadequate
to sustain robust health.
Despite the saving ministrations
we made to whomever asked of us
we owned our own liabilities.
Castillo suffered a persistent cough
and Dorantes, Estevanico and I
each succumbed to short bouts of fever.
After some doubtful discussion

Dorantes offered a pragmatic solution:
he decreed we must eat meat
if we were to garner sufficient strength
to undertake our planned journey.
But the only flesh at hand
hung from the scrawny dogs
that skulked on the village outskirts.
Despite our standing as miracle-makers
it took Dorantes two soft deer skins
to persuade the tribe's esteemed chieftain
that we should take dogs for our purpose.

Only long after darkness had fallen
and the tribesmen were soundly sleeping
did Dorantes and Estevanico
select the three healthiest curs
kill them in silent suffocation
and prepare them for roasting on embers.
We each took turns fitfully resting
as the meat tantalizingly sizzled.
For four weeks no meat had passed our lips.
We feared the smell would wake
our prone Indian companions
and we would be forced to thinly share
that which we needed to stoutly march
to the farthest western coast.
So it was that we each took
just two savoury mouthfuls of dog flesh
wrapped what remained in leaves
and silently crept from the village
long before dawn touched the sky.
The meat served its purpose.
Two days later we felt positively light-limbed
as we issued from the dank forest
and turned our feet towards the setting sun.
But if we thought our new journey

would be spent in weeks of solitude
we reckoned too little with man.
Word proceeded our presence.

The first tribespeople we met
knew of us and our powers
and would brook no refusals
as they took us by our hands
and led us to their villages.
I still vividly recall what thoughts
struck me when we walked
between scrawny skin-stitched lodges
and looked into the radiant faces
of equally scrawny Indian children.
I felt myself in the midst of a ritual
which followed an age-old pattern
as firmly cast as any religious rite.
First we were importuned
with a flurry of pleas and wringing hands.
Next we were led in solemn procession
to the place the tribe considered sacred
where we were seated in honour
and required to watch patiently
as they laid out for us their best food.
After the repast was devoured
the ailing were introduced
that we might terminate wretchedness
and make a heaven of their lives.
All occurred among repeated entreaties
that proclaimed us sons of the Sun God
sent to help them endure
the rigours and pains of their lives.
It might be thought such aggrandizing
would inflate our sense of self-worth.
The opposite occurred.

I have already written of
the self-doubting depths Castillo fell into
fearing all this to be the Devil's work
an evil trap set to plunge his soul
into the fiercest fires of Hell.
By now he prayed more for himself
craving God forgive his flaws
than he did blessing the beseeching sick.
Dorantes and Estevanico proved
equally impervious to flattery.
In their shared pragmatic stance
they considered they stood in the wash
Castillo stirred as he did the work
God had picked out for him.
And if they at all sparkled
it was not of their own making
but Castillo's cast off effervescence.
For myself I saw the reverence
the tribespeople projected onto us
was more than ever could be due
to any who wear a human frame.
Yet our being proclaimed
the sons of the Indian's Sun God
hurt Castillo's heart greatly.
He thought our powers were given us
to prove to benighted savages
that our Christian God was superior
to all their natural superstitions.
Yet was God so filled with self-doubt
that He required us to bolster
His impoverished image of Himself
by impressing a few thousand Indians?
I preferred to think it was from love
that He helped whoever was in want
and we had become instruments
not to prove His superiority

but to embody His compassion.
In this, as with many other such thoughts
Castillo and I knelt on opposed knees.

θ θ θ

That same night, after we had healed
all the ailing of this newly-met tribe
a large group of women arrived
from a village further along our way.
Having travelled many leagues
they were exhausted and wished to rest.
Our hosts similarly sought of us
that we stay the following day
and feast with them to celebrate
the healing of their ill.
Yet we had rested too many months
and no longer wished to be held
from our long-planned journey.
So although we were ourselves tired
we waited for the tribespeople to sleep
then continued on our way.
Crossing the cactus-stubbled savanna
it was plain we would not now starve
there being many ripening prickly pears.
What was not plain was the path.
Come dawn the mountains were as distant
as they had been from the village.
We feared we had circled, not progressed.
Of course not knowing where you are
is never the same as being lost.
And we soon found ourselves
embarked on a fascinating new phase
of this our ever surprising journey.

16 A New Custom Arises

NO MAN at birth can know
what the mature years of his life
will lead him into or reveal.
Perhaps this ignorance is required
for if we knew what pain would be our lot
who would happily walk towards the future?
Yet if we could avoid all pain
what would our life become?
A pleasant life. A predictable life.
But a brave life? A stimulating life?
A life that manifests our power
to sow and reap our God-given talents?
I here attest my conviction
that all the challenges I faced
made me stronger and bolder:
they made me more than I otherwise am.
This for me is the purpose of life:
not seeking the worst of nature and man
but unflinchingly wrestling it when it comes.
For we then draw on cloaked reserves
and extend ourselves far beyond
our bare unlearned mewling selves
to more become all we might be.
I assert this my insubstantial philosophy
as prologue to what occurred next.

At noon the women we left behind
found us resting beside a spring.
They were greatly agitated
as they had sought us since dawn.
For ourselves we had lost the path.

We walked a futile four leagues
circling back to where we had departed
and were now grateful to follow their lead.
We trekked four hours to a wide river
then waded through chest high water
using branches to balance against the current.
At sunset we discovered why
the women had been so anxious to find us.
Approaching a village of one hundred lodges
we were confronted by a surging horde
who slapped their thighs and shouted
as if to frighten ghosts and ghouls.
Some carried gourds they rattled violently.
We learned later these gourds
had been drilled and filled with pebbles
being shaken to effect blessings and cures
the efficacy of which resulted
from their having fallen from heaven.
Such a heaven-made claim was often made
on behalf of the most unlikely objects.
Yet such statements we never belittled
for did not Moses and his wanderers
eat of manna that fell from heaven?
And is not heaven the home of angels?
And do we not own hopes of dwelling there
once we cast off this encumbering body?
In truth our survival in these harsh lands
was due to the tribespeople believing
we were inflated by heaven's nurturing breath.

Whether they thought us heaven-sent or no
our presence so excited these Indians
they snatched us off our feet
and carried us bodily to their lodges.
Fearing injury from such boisterousness
we remained shut in the lodges assigned us

refusing to emerge while all night outside
the Indians feasted, danced and sang.
Surely they were not carousing
but rather expressing their joy
at the heavens having blessed them?
I felt my observation confirmed
when at dawn we emerged from the lodges
and were met in reverent silence.
After a breakfast of roasted prickly pears
our long day's work began.
We prayed for, breathed upon, and signed
the cross over the heads of all present.
We remained a day in that village
bequeathing the healing of heaven
on all who craved curing.
They later verified they were healed.
We left the following dawn.
But we could not do so alone.
The entire tribe it seemed
accompanied us to the next village
that lay on our path to the mountains.
It was then a new custom occurred.

Θ Θ Θ

We were expected.
As we entered this new village
our hosts were lined in respectful rows.
Their chief then commanded treasures
be reverently placed at our feet:
arrows, bows, beads, skins and shoes.
Our practice had long been to reassign
such offerings among all present.
But before we made any move
those who had guided us here
stepped in and swept it all away.

Our new hosts burst out wailing
making much show that their gifts
were for the sons of Heaven
not for low thieving Indians.
But with their own bows and arrows
now turned upon them
they were helpless to prevent
our guides entering their huts
and taking corn and ground meal.
The thieves then departed at a trot
bearing all they could carry.
Our hosts were inconsolable.
Even our healing ministrations
satisfied them but a few hours.
However when we left next morning
they appeared reconciled to their loss.
Chattering, laughing and singing
the entire tribe accompanied us
on our trek to the next village.
Late that day we discovered why.
For when the next villagers
laid their treasures before us
our companions took everything.
They then departed laughing
saying our hosts should do the same
to those in the next village we entered.

We were as distraught at this new turn
as the robbed and weeping Indians.
Yet despite our spirited status
perpetrators and victims both
ignored our objections
and this new custom was deployed
in the next villages we entered.
We again attempted intervention.
We were again ignored.

This same pattern was repeated
in village after village.
Thus was a noble service
tainted by grasping human greed.
When at last we reached a desert
we determined to alter our journey.
The Indians told us none lived
in the barren wilderness wastes
and wished us to walk another direction
where they said many other tribes lived.
But this was not towards the setting sun.
We ignored their pleas
and next morning entered the desert.
The Indians refused to accompany us
fearing lack of water and food
telling us we surely would die.
That day we thought they spoke true
for we found neither prickly pears
nor anything else to consume.
But late on the second day
we spied spiralling smoke
and soon came on twenty lodges
sited on the banks of a small river.
The wonder was not that we found them
but that even these knew of us
for on spying our approach
they burst into lamentation and weeping.
Clearly they knew whoever we met
would be plundered of all they owned.
But when they realised we were alone
their fear swiftly dissolved to joy.
Eagerly they laid beans and corn before us
plus treasured arrows, bows and beads.
They then implored that we heal their aches.
We gladly did as they desired
and that night enjoyed a sound sleep.

But next dawn we woke to shouts.
It seemed those we left at the desert edge
now surrounded all the lodges
and demanded reward for sending us here.
Only when they had been delivered
of gourds filled with beans and corn
and had snatched up
all the bows and arrows they could carry
did they depart back to their village.

Of course no nation monopolises
the ever-attendant human traits
of deviousness, dishonesty, deceit
and all those common traits
that erect in this our God-given world
hovels of human-made horror.
Only the desert that stretched before us
offered refuge from duplicity.
The Indians implored us not to go there
saying there was nothing to eat or drink
for seventeen days of walking.
They commended we instead trek up-river
where lay many villages and treasures.
Of course that was the direction
in which they could make good their loss.
We declined their urgings.
Instead we gathered water and dried corn
then left them wailing
as we walked into the wilderness.
We truly were what the Indians said of us:
dead men trekking into
a shimmering fever of stones, dust, heat.

17 Flying Among Eagles

W E DISCOVERED to our misfortune
no duplicity in the Indians' claim
the desert lacked food for seventeen days.
I shall not recount our suffering
as we traversed that barren land.
But we survived.
When we emerged from the wavering heat
and stepped onto the mountains' foothills
we must have presented a fearsome sight:
our bodies were naked
our hair matted with sweat and filth
bones boldly protruded beneath our skin.
Coated in dust we must have appeared
more ghosts than men.
I assert this because the first people we met
were women who threw down their baskets
and ran shrieking from us to their village.
We followed more sedately.
Indeed it was all we could manage
to remain upright on our feet
and sustain forward momentum.
When the village men met us
we showed them our bleeding feet
to convince them we were men not ghouls.
They invited us to eat and rest with them.
This generosity was the counter-balance
to the thievery we lately had encountered.
Alas, one season each year they ate straw
and we had arrived in that season!
Yet straw is a feast to the starved

and so it surely would have proved
had our stomachs been able to digest it.
Instead we joked about our generosity
in not taking the little they possessed
from the mouths of destitute Indians.
Rarely were we able to be so generous!
So began the next phase of our journey.

θ θ θ

As we advanced into the mountains
we discovered new Indian tribes
and their ever novel customs.
A surprising find was the first houses
we ever saw among these transient tribes.
Some were built from mud bricks
others cleverly constructed of cane matting
that hung from an armature of branches.
We enquired of those living in them
if they had seen such houses elsewhere
perhaps built by men who looked like us.
Their response was an indifferent shrug.
They had been born into them
and possessed no sense of their history
but that they had always existed.
Among all New World Indians
we found this same lack of enquiry
regarding their origin and antiquity.
Yet these people were well-formed
carried themselves with dignity
and cultivated crops of beans and squash
among thin fields of corn.
They also practised a curious custom
I never witnessed elsewhere.
Possessing no cooking pots

they prepared food by first filling
a medium-sized gourd with water
then heated stones in a fire
and dropped them into the gourd.
The process was repeated
until the water began boiling.
They then took out the stones
and threw in whatever they wished to cook.
Such is human inventiveness
that overcomes life deficiencies.
Our progress now became swift.
The mountains were cooler than the plains
and we walked unhindered between villages.
At first none knew who we were
so we were not paused by requests to heal.
But a singular event dramatically altered
the way we were known and perceived.

Ө Ө Ө

By this time we thought we had seen
all this vast land contained.
Yet each day is a chance to taste anew
the wondrous and remarkable.
Our next striking encounter
occurred late one afternoon
as we neared a village on a small plateau.
We were alone for the plains custom
of walking us to the next village
was unknown and so unpracticed here.
The sun stood low in the sky
casting hot light across the mud huts
and making deep shadows of the rest.
But as we wearily approached
what struck us most was the quiet.

We were used to the sounds of tribal life
similar to those of a Spanish village:
people shouting and laughing
the striking of stones in grinding
children running and screaming
the growling and barking of dogs
ended in yelping when struck by stones.
Yet here we heard no human voices
nor the noise of human activity—
just the almost inaudible whir of wind
as it whipped up a spiral of dust
then died away into stillness.

We entered the village cautiously
for there was always the danger
of stumbling into what may be regretted.
There we found twelve men and women
seated silently in a semi-circle.
Their clothes declared them uncommon.
We knew each tribe had chiefs and elders
who memorised their people's history
perpetuated ancient customs
and enforced the laws they all lived by.
Some chiefs wore the skins of animals
others beads or gaudy head dresses
all to advertise their elevated status.
These Indians were not of such stock.
Most wore bones hung in necklaces
or decorating their hair or nose.
Others had painted faces and chests
red, yellow and black lines
spirals of purple and blue.
These were medicine men and women
brujos and brujas reputed to make magic
to cast spells, cure the sick and injured

and who inhabited the twilight world
that shimmers between life and death.
Such at least was what we heard.
We halted short of the gathering.
The most wrinkled and grave brujo
was seated at the group's head.
He signalled us to step forwards.
A gap in the semi-circle was sited
so we might sit and exactly close the circle.
Clearly, our presence was anticipated.

At such times Estevanico spoke for us
as he unravelled all Indian languages.
We were asked why we had come
and said we sought to join our countrymen
who lived on the distant western coast.
We asked how they knew we would come
and one brujo was pointed out
as possessing the eyes and wings of an eagle.
He had witnessed our desert journey.
We asked if he possessed an eyeglass
that he could stand on a mountain peak
and peer at us crawling far below.
Their response was a ripple of laughter.
No further explanation was offered.
It was an ambiguity that sustained
that strange encounter
all fed by an otherworldly silence.
We were used to babbling village voices
as many simultaneously sought our regard.
Here one spoke at a time
and calm eyes gazed deep into ours
enquiring, weighing, evaluating.
The last time I had witnessed such intent
was many years before

when Castillo and I were first captured
and our threatened lives were saved
by a sagacious medicine man.
We enquired why they waited for us
and what it was they sought.
The Indian who appeared their elder
replied they had witnessed our healing
and all wished to meet the remarkable brujos
who had come from across the seas.
This claim caused us considerable confusion.
Over this past eventful year
thousands had received our healing touch.
Yet we had not seen striking Indians like these.
When asked how they observed our acts
given we had never met them before
the chief brujo pointed to Dorantes
and stated he had perceived their presence.
We turned to Dorantes: he shrugged.
Yet he later admitted he remembered
seeing these Indians in dreams that began
the time Castillo healed the hundreds
in the cactus fields of prickly pears.
The brujo now said of Dorantes
that he was a knowledge dreamer.
Dreamers came in different kinds.
Dorantes' skill was to be given in dreams
knowledge of plants' subtle powers
and of hidden human motives and desires.
Pointing to the Negro Estevanico
the brujo called him a shape-shifter
whose facility with languages
and ease with all kinds of people
reflected his skill to be other than he was.
Indeed he used his size and dark skin
as garments to disguise himself

that none should see his true self.
Estevanico was told that with training
he could greatly increase his powers
and that the dreamer Dorantes
could uncover what he needed to know.
Indeed those two had joined their lives
so their separate skills might bloom
as a result of mutual endeavour.
Turning to Castillo and myself
the brujo said we were heavenly gourds.
We had done much to empty ourselves
that healing power might flow through us.
More draining would facilitate greater prowess.
He concluded that we four had survived
where all our companions had not
because we each possessed a competence
that came from an unearthly source.
He smiled as he stated this
adding they had witnessed our efforts
to draw from beyond what we lacked on Earth.

These words were suggestive and beguiling.
They made sense of what we had experienced
during our New World adventures.
Yet their unChristian prospect was troubling.
I recognised Castillo's inward bristling.
I have since debated the brujo's words
at great length with Dorantes
and thought much myself on their import.
The brujo's terms and perspective were alien
and parcelled perceptions I never heard told
in any Christian country I travelled.
Yet is strangeness reason to reject anything?
Heaven is a realm none knows.
It is alien to our experience

yet we hope for it every day of our lives.
If we reject all that is alien and baffling
how will we ever arrive at the new?
As God created the world and all in it
is not everything new dispensed by His Hand?
So why do we run from a novel notion
yet turn towards that unknown we call Heaven
(that may be quite alien to what we think)
except through fear, ignorance, self-care
and a desire to conform to the approved?
All this has much occupied my heart
over the years that followed that meeting.

The brujo ceased speaking as dusk fell.
We assumed we had heard what was intended
because fires were lit and we all ate together.
Then one among them began to beat a drum.
Fragrant herbs were thrown on the flames
and in the flickering orange firelight
each brujo and bruja danced in turn.
This was not the jumping and shaking
of those we had long lived among.
These were more mysterious.
We observed them dancing as animals:
a crow with sharp beak and hungry gaze
a lizard slithering among rocks
a slender and delicately stepping deer
a large cat with yellow coat and black eyes.
Their movements were so well emulated
it seemed the brujos and brujas embodied
whatever animal they chose.
I make no claim to know what occurred
but I avouch that more than human shapes
danced around us that unique night.
And the world around us responded.

We heard the quiet snuffling, flapping, pawing
of creatures that remained beyond the light.
This provided yet another instance
of the mystery that surrounds us.
With my companions I was raised
to treat nature as my handmaiden
whose wares were wholly for my benefit.
All living in nature was our inferior
given us by God to dig, cut, kill and transform
for our superior human intent and use.
Our priests dressed in the finest
we plundered from the bounteous Earth
wearing moneyed gowns to prove
man's taming of the God-bestowed world.
In contrast these Indian priests
wore not gold and silver thread
but the bones of admired animals
that were not gruesome ornaments of death
but celebrated that all creatures carry gifts
given them by the Divine.
Thus they choose to make of the world
not a pasture, mine or abattoir
but a church in which they daily worshipped.
Such at least is my surmise.

When the evocative dancing ceased
and the fanned fires burned down
we retired to assigned lodges.
Despite the distance we had walked
I felt refreshed not exhausted.
For some time I lay awake
feeling the velvet night around me.
I remember hearing wings softly flutter.
Next morning Castillo said he heard bats.
But there were none present in my lodge.

When I did finally sleep
I felt I fell into a rich darkness
that held me as in subtle down.
And I dreamed I rode the wind
high above that mountain village
seeing the ground below illuminated
by an unearthly golden glow
like a candle might cast through a veil.
Over plains and villages and lakes I flew
feeling an unfettered freedom
such that I had never before experienced.
I felt at one time I did not fly alone
and heard in response a bird cry beside me.
Yet I lacked the power to turn and look.
So I gave myself wholly over to the pleasure
of wings, wind, flying and freedom.

Ɵ Ɵ Ɵ

When we woke next morning
we found fresh food and water.
But all the Indians had vanished.
However one final incident
ended this curious encounter.
We were on a mountain path.
Far below us was a green forested valley
in which a snaking silver river glinted.
Come noon we arrived at a pass
from which three paths branched.
One clearly descended to the valley.
But we could not decide which
of the other two best suited our purpose.
As we stood discussing our choice
an eagle swooped down and landed
on a rock not far from us.

It stared at us intently for a time
allowing us to view its orange face
white neck and black body and wings.
I recognised the colours as the same
as those painted on the head bruja's face.
The bird then lifted off the rock
and flew above one of the two paths.
It hovered a time in the wind
then made a cry and flew off.
Dorantes jokingly asked of Castillo
whether God or Devil had given us a sign.
Castillo made no response.
He had been powerfully shaken
by the previous day's meeting with the Indians.
They were undoubtedly much more
than mere dabblers in herbs and healing
such as practised by common medicine men.
But whether their power was black or white
much concerned Castillo.
The answer was not easily discerned
but I myself felt no threat from them
nor any desire to overpower or harm us.
Rather I saw demeanours
filled with other-worldly concerns.
And I saw dreams drift behind their eyes
dreams of this world
yet uncommon and viewed aslant
as if by sight that was more than human.

18 A Dead Man Walks

As WE TREKKED across this land
it seemed word of us
walked well ahead of our feet.
I say this because we now discovered
a novel custom asserted itself.
When we entered a village
we were not met by waiting Indians.
Instead they sat silent in their lodges
facing the walls with heads bowed
hair pulled over their faces
and all possessions piled
in the centres of their dwellings.
Only after we gave greeting
and returned them their property
did they relax and shyly ask for healing.
Not wishing to repeat the stealing
that so disturbed us on the plains
we adopted a new strategy.
We now deliberately stayed distant
not speaking to any who approached us.
Instead all questions and responses
we directed through Estevanico.
Thus we hoped to retain authority
and the power to promote just relations
between one tribe and the next.
Whether our gambit truly worked
or if these Indians were merely fairer
than those thieves who occupied the plains
we never plainly concluded.
However we made happier progress.
Using Estevanico as our sole voice

to clarify which paths were fastest and best
we made rapid passage to the west
walking through fruitful mountain valleys
and ever chasing the setting sun.

Cattle were so plentiful in this region
and skins and cloaks proved so numerous
we named these people Tribes of the Cow.
In appreciation of our healing skills
we were gifted too many hides to carry
giving them instead to whomever we met.
Indeed we preferred to travel naked.
After years of that attire
we were well immured to the seasons
and our prior sufferings had trained us
so well that nothing daunted our travel.
If any tribes proclaimed no food
lay in the direction we chose to walk
we prepared ourselves to fast.
The Indians much marvelled
that we ate so little and walked so far.
We took to carrying deer tallow
and supping from each day's portion.
This sustained us in our journey.
What fed my heart was seeing
women much better treated here
without the incessant beatings
that always caused me to quail within.
These women wore knee-length cotton shirts
loosely fastened at front with string
and over that a half-sleeved jacket
made of scraped deerskin
with low hanging tasselled strips.
Their feet were protected by shoes.
When our escorting women gave birth
they always demanded we touch

and sign the cross over their newborn.
My companions sometimes grew vexed
at fulfilling such dogged invitations.
But I greatly enjoyed these occasions
happily bouncing a baby on my knee
and gazing into its opaque eyes—
for much joy lies in celebrating
the birth of a newborn being.
My pleasure lay in pondering what future
would unfold for this helpless babe.
Would it always remain helpless?
Or would it shape life to its will?
Would its will be broken by life
or would life and will dance in unison?
And would that dancing be for good or ill?
Naturally it is futile to ask questions
only implacable time can answer.
I pondered them nonetheless.
Our puzzle as human beings
resides not in that we are
but in the powers we possess within
and what we may blossom into.
This continual heart-felt unfolding
is the true mystery that drives
our quest to comprehend our being.

However our mundane reality was
we often felt ourselves too pressed
due to the relentless presence
of all the men and women who walked us
from their village to the next.
That they sought our touch and approval
became at times a trying burden.
One night for our own tranquility
we left the lodges we were assigned
and walked into the fields.

The weather being warm
we spent some time talking.
It was a pleasure we rarely experienced
given we were silent when accompanied
and that was every waking hour.
Our respite was brief.
We were soon hunted out
by alarmed tribespeople
who worried they had offended us.
We feigned anger in order to hold them
some distance from us
that we might pretend to be alone.
A strange coincidence then followed.

The next day an Indian woman
came down with a sudden illness.
She died a handful of hours later.
But before she did many others
similarly fell to the ground
unable to stand or speak.
They too soon started dying.
In the face of this disaster our care failed.
The Indians implored we tell them
how they had neglected to love us.
They begged we lift our curse
from their stricken populace—
for they linked our recent anger
with this death-dealing pestilence.
To prove their enduring love
they brought us more treasure:
luxuriously woven cotton blankets
better than any I saw in New Spain
and exquisitely fashioned arrows
the heads of which were emerald.
In truth, we were as desperate as the Indians
to relieve them of their wretchedness.

To this end we spent the night in prayer
asking God to lift this baffling plague.
Next day far fewer fell ill.
By the third day the pestilence abated.
But before we could continue
yet another unexpected event occurred.

Early on the third morning
after the scourge first struck
two terrified women approached us
craving we attend to an elder
lying ill in the next village.
Our local Indians were recovering
and Castillo was exhausted.
So I took Dorantes and Estevanico
and together we followed their lead.
But when we arrived the man was dead.
We perceived this because
the Indians were weeping
and the man's hut was torn down
as is customary when an occupant dies.
Dorantes removed the covering mat
placed over the elder to keep off flies
and we jointly examined the dead man.
His eyeballs were rolled back
and we felt no pulse at his neck or wrist.
Nonetheless I knelt by the corpse
and asked the Lord to enact His will.
My companions patiently waited
as I spent an hour in prayer.
In truth, after that first request
I spent the remainder rapt in silence
transported out of myself
into a realm of calm enchantment.
Eventually I relaxed and stood.
After breathing on the corpse

and additionally signing the cross
I did the same to all who were ill.
We three then rejoined Castillo.
I thought no more of the incident.
But next morning we woke to excitement.
It seemed the dead man had revived
risen from his bed
shrugged off his shroud
and was now eating, drinking and talking.
The others I attended
had recovered too from their ills.
This occasion generated much awe.
For myself I make no claim.
But our reputation in the mountains swelled
and we were offered so much food and goods
an army would be required to carry it.
It was leading a triumphal procession
that we now strode from village to village.
And it was in one of these villages
a mere huddle of mud houses
seemingly hung from rocky crags
that we received a reassuring sign.

19 The Destitute Plain

WHY IS IT we most fear
       what we most desire?
I ask this question now because
at that time the feeling rose in me
that we would soon meet Christians.
Of course it was in hope of such an end
we had crossed from the eastern coast.
So why did this feeling make me uneasy?
Did my heart possess knowledge
my mind could not access?
I have never believed in foretelling.
Yet I remember a striking occasion
early in our New World expedition
when we first arrived in Cuba
to replenish our depleted foodstocks
and a soldier's wife refused to embark.
She claimed that in a vision she saw
our fleet of five vessels sink.
She first attempted to persuade her own
and others' husbands to abandon our voyage.
When this strategy proved fruitless
she stirred many wives with such fears
that they abandoned their husbands
and took local men for companions.
Our departure was delayed for more days
than we desired as we sought to reconcile
angry husbands and distraught wives.
Eventually we had no choice
but to abandon the recalcitrant women.
During our first days sailing at sea
my men snorted at their wives' madness.

But when storms split our fleet
the repudiating laughter dried.
And when our ships sank one by one
there was much venomous speculation
some malevolent spirit had whispered
in the gullible women's ears
or even that they were witches
culpable for our expedition's dire plight.

I do not know how it could be
that woman knew what she did.
I certainly refuse to anoint
natural events with supernatural origin.
However many do condemn as Devil's work
whatever makes a misery of their lives
or has a cause they do not comprehend.
To this day I remain curious
about such strange ways of knowing.
For the truth is fleeting feelings and dreams
have indeed informed me in advance
of events that played out as fore-felt.
Yet this makes me neither a prognosticator
nor the Devil's boon companion.
It is rather another form of knowing
that scoffers or cynics may readily dismiss
yet is not thereby explained away.
Indeed my own feeling we would soon
come upon Christians proved correct
as did my inward doubt that
made me fear what I truly desired.
The first, at least, I heartily welcomed.

ɵ ɵ ɵ

We traversed a mountain peak
and entered a rock-strewn pass

our Indians said led to the plains below.
We were impatient to descend
but entered the village perched there
and instead with equanimity performed
the requested blessings and healings.
Thereafter Dorantes was gifted
six hundred hearts of deer.
They had been preserved by cooking
so their taste did not offend.
Yet their presence certainly did.
I could not but contemplate the fates
of those six hundred deer
that now provided a savoury luxury.
What orgy of killing had ended their lives?
Were all the carcasses stripped, dried, used?
Or was there indifferent human wastage?
Alive to the irony of the heartless killing
we called this place the Village of Hearts.
However such was my aversion to excess
I declined to partake of the gift.
Besides our stomachs were
little accustomed to such richness.
So after nibbling a handful for show
my three companions fed all the hearts
to those who accompanied us.
They much appreciated what we could not.
It was during the distribution
that we received our next significant sign.
On a leather thong hung from an Indian's neck
Castillo spied a small metal sword buckle
woven with a horseshoe nail.
He nonchalantly sought of the Indian
how he came to be wearing this ornament.
The owner said it had fallen from Heaven.
Further questioning wrung from others
that they were left by bearded men like us

who had come from heaven riding horses
and armed with lances and swords.
They had killed two from this very village
and when they left took food and women.
Such was our reintroduction
to our brave and noble countrymen.

Θ Θ Θ

The plains were hot but fertile.
Three kinds of deer grazed there
one the size of Castilian calves.
The people lived in mudbrick huts
and cropped corn and beans thrice a year.
This was well because our companions
now numbered in their hundreds.
The first village we approached
enacted the familiar ritual
of greeting us and offering food
which we together contentedly ate.
We then blessed their sick
and watched them dance and sing.
All this occupied a day and a night.
When the inhabitants of a second village
appeared next dawn before us
laden with food and treasures
the whole cycle was repeated.
Then again for yet another visiting village.
Only on the fifth morning did we leave.
Many more days passed before we finally
reached the western coast
and stood on a cliff top
looking down at the distant crawling ocean.
It was an occasion we savoured
knowing our presence here
was a victory for tenacity and luck

underpinned by God's mercy.
Yet we saw no signs of galleons
nor heard recent reports
of Spanish sails plowing the swell.
We then had a decision to make.
The coast extended north and south
yet we could walk but one direction.
Enquiry brought us knowledge
these plains stretched a thousand leagues.
Yet villages stood more thickly to the south.
We each felt the south was best likely
to reveal the presence of our countrymen.
So with that orientation we walked.

Hope and despair are boon companions.
Finding one soon brought us the other.
But we were first delayed
fifteen days by a swollen river.
When the waters fell sufficiently to cross
numerous of our Indians also fell away.
Despite their joy at travelling with us
they refused to progress further south.
We soon discovered why.
The first village we entered was empty.
Over the following weeks
village after village told the same dire tale
of desertion and destruction.
Dwellings were roofless and fire-blackened.
Mud ovens were kicked apart.
Half burnt blankets and broken gourds
lay strewn in haphazard wreckage.
Cropped fields lay abandoned.
The few Indians who still walked with us
said all had withdrawn to the mountains
to escape Christian scavenging and killing.
Of course we were encouraged

because these signs of Christian presence
fanned our hope of finding our countrymen.
Our despair was the signs were so ugly.
As we progressed across the plain
we felt keening sorrow hung over the land.
Perhaps this was our projection
for guilt certainly gripped us as we
contemplated our countrymen's grim work.
But our walking became an opportunity
to contemplate how we might prevent
what our uneasy Indians clearly feared
would be done to them again and again.

As we proceeded down the coast
we ate whatever occasion brought us.
Guavas and figs we plucked from wild trees.
At times we found in shattered villages
corn stored in unbroken gourds
that vermin had not nosed out before us.
Twice Dorantes and Indian hunters
caught deer we roasted on spits.
But it was in quiet moments I best feasted.
I remember lying on beach sands
enfolded by a warm autumn night
watching the pin-bright stars wheel
across an otherwise jet-black sky.
I hugged the vast hanging over my head
and thanked God who made me man.
All this fed my grateful heart.
Reflecting now on my life's journey
I cannot but wonder if that feeding
was shaped for me at the date of my birth.
Is our personal future an ordained path
that neither choice nor accident
ever diverts our feet from following?
Or is our future uncharted even by fate

so the path we walk day by day
is shaped by choice, chance and the mystery
that feeds and nurtures our life?
Such occasions and my thinking on them
have sustained me over the many lean years
when I doubted I had much future at all.
Of course the oncoming slows for no man.
The next days of our future soon arrived.

θ θ θ

Signs of Christian presence appeared:
horseshoe impressions in dried mud
and wooden stakes to tether horses
driven into the yielding earth.
But none were recently hewn.
We then met trekking Indians
who declared they had seen
men on horseback seven days before.
The encounter occurred inland
in jungle towards the mountains.
We sought to persuade them
to guide us to the place of encounter.
They refused and declared
we could not want to meet such monsters.
When we argued we were men
just like those we sought
they shook their heads and laughed.
They had seen dressed men riding horses
while we were naked and travelled on foot.
And our Indians were free companions
while their Indians walked in chains.
When they proved impervious to persuasion
we took direction from them and walked
towards the distant mountain range.
We soon caught sight of hunched Indians

who preferred jungle swamps and boggy ground
where Spanish horses could not step.
At this time we found abandoned remains
of a dozen Christian encampments
but none showed fresh ashes or horse dung.
By now we had gathered a retinue
of perhaps one hundred Indians.
Some among them now begged us
to visit their families and tribespeople
to heal them and refresh their hearts.
We happily answered their hopes.
In three days we re-entered the mountains
and ascended a steep pass to a village
hidden among the crags.
In a small village of fifty huts
two thousand people now sheltered
having fled the countryside below
abandoning their crops and villages
from fear of being killed or enslaved.
All had lost family to the marauders
for such our feared countrymen were named.
With their crops abandoned
food was replaced by fear, hunger, illness.
There was in our ministerings
more need to heal hearts than bodies.
We did both.
Our joy was that in our honour
concealed food was laid before us
which we distributed among all.
Yet we apprehended more than a meal
was needed to mend these broken people.

Ө Ө Ө

At dawn the forest is raucous
with bird song and furtive slithering

through quivering leaves and undergrowth.
We led two hundred Indians
to the thinning edges of the jungle.
As a group we availed each other safety:
with us at their head they feared no Christians
while their numbers would protect us
if we ever met Indians set to avenge
the deaths caused by marauding foreigners.
We finally discovered fresh horse dung.
Dorantes calculated a Christian band
was no more than three days away.
Suddenly all Indian bravado died
as they proclaimed they had no passion
to meet our predatory compatriots.
So with Estevanico I took a handful
of the most daring braves.
In one day we trekked ten leagues
and found three overnight Christian camps.
Next morning I achieved that goal
my companions and I had long hoped for
yet equally had come to fear.

20 A Christian Welcome

THE CHRISTIANS' surprise was palpable
when I stepped from the jungle
followed by the black-skinned Estevanico.
Four Christians on horseback stared at me
their mouths gaping, not speaking a word.
I don't know what disconcerted them more:
my attire (which consisted of my nakedness)
or that with me was an unclothed Negro
and ten armed Indian warriors.
I watched reactions flitting across their faces
as they wondered if they were seeing right.
I saved them from their dilemma
by walking slowly towards them
greeting them in bowing courtly Spanish
and asking to meet their commander.
By noon I was in his presence.
His name was Diego de Alcazar
and he was as perplexed as his soldiers.
I explained my history and circumstance.
He responded he was sorely troubled
because the Indians had taken to hiding
leaving their fields and crops abandoned.
Not only had he captured no Indians
but with no food to trade or claim
his men were sliding towards starvation.
He sought of me as a Christian
to help him gain the Indians' trust
that he might progress his mission
and feed his dispirited men.
I told him ten leagues at our rear
Castillo and Dorantes waited my word.

With them were two hundred Indians
while thousands more awaited our signal
that they might descend from the mountains
and return to their villages and fields.
Before I spoke any further
Alcazar commanded three men mount
and seek out my two companions.
They took ten freed Indians with them
to show his Christian intent was harmless.
Estevanico led them as guide.

ɵ ɵ ɵ

Five days later Dorantes and Castillo
arrived at Commander Alcazar's camp.
With them were six hundred Indians.
Alcazar promptly asked us to command
the Indians bring his men supplies.
But there was no need.
Unbidden the Indians brought more food
than we and Alcarzar's men could consume.
For the first night in weeks
our Spanish compatriots slept replete.
But Alcazar was not so easily appeased.
Next morning he demanded we surrender
our attendant Indians to his command.
We thought to blunt his avarice
by giving him many calf-skin cloaks
that had in turn been presented us.
Alcazar and his voracious men
grabbed what we gave ungracefully
then insisted again on their right to captives.
Much arguing followed.
The Commander claimed it was our duty
to serve our religion and King
and so aid him in his occupation and charge.

[164]

But we vehemently would not allow
anyone with us to be placed in chains.
Alcazar then accused us of favouring savages
over good God-fearing Christians.
At this we decided to debate him no further
preferring silence over futile speech.
The cunning Commander then shifted tack.
Ordering a captured Indian to translate
he informed all the tribespeople
that we four had shamefully deserted
our religion and countrymen.
He declared us heartless renegades
where he and his men were noble Christians
who must be suitably served and obeyed.
All the while he spoke the Indians ignored him
preferring to talk and laugh among themselves.

When he was done speechifying
one among the Indians stepped forth
and proclaimed Alcazar lied.
His rationale was unequivocal.
We four had walked out of the sunrise
whereas Alcazar's men came from sunset.
We were naked, had nothing and walked on foot
while the Christians wore elaborate clothing
rode horses and carried long lances.
We healed the sick where they killed the healthy.
And we not only asked for nothing
but gave away all we were presented
while the Christians had no aim
but to plunder all they could snatch
and never gave what they possessed to anyone.
Indeed such was the contrast they drew
between us and Alcazar and his men
we were never able to convince them
we were all of the same lands and religion.

Only after much gesturing and signs
did we convince them to leave us there
and return to their own people.
Yet this was not the end of Alcazar's tricks.
He next promised to relent and protect
those Indians who returned to the plains
and revived their villages and crops.
To that end Alcazar introduced to us
a conniving magistrate named Cebreros.
On the pretext we should visit hiding Indians
and reassure them they would be protected
if they returned to cultivate their lands
this Cebreros took us deep into the jungle.
We made such tardy progress
that for two days we wandered without water
sighting neither trails nor signs of habitation.
Conditions proved so bad seven men died
from among the Christians and their captives.
To our despair we later discovered
while we were cut off from our Indian friends
Alcazar and his men struck them down.
Fifty were taken into chained custody
with eleven wounded and two killed outright.
Cebreros' purpose was to distract us.
After trekking twenty-five difficult leagues
we at last entered a quiet village
where Indians happily served the Christians.
By now suspecting we had been played
but not yet knowing Alcazar's ploy
we sought of Cebreros that he
introduce us to his distraught Indians.
Instead of responding
he mounted a horse and left us to ourselves.

θ θ θ

Melchor Diaz was chief magistrate
of that far-flung province.
Based in the small town of Culiacan
he came swiftly to meet us the moment
Cebreros informed him of our presence.
He greeted us with kisses and largesse
and made much of our shipwrecked years
praising God that we survived our ordeal.
When we proved less attentive to praise
and more inclined to describe
how the equivocators Alcazar and Cebreros
had treated us and our Indian companions
he indignantly declared in both his name
and in that of Governor Nuño de Guzman
he would redeem each ill done to all.

Next morning the Governor arrived.
We wished to progress to Mexico City
but he implored us to remain.
His problem proved the same as Alcazar's:
the countryside was empty
and with fertile land uncultivated
the purpose of occupation was blunted.
For who can work without food?
The Governor's purpose was to uncover
and extract metals from the land.
This could not effectively be done
when his men were chasing natives.
He then sought to convince us
we would serve both our King and religion
by persuading the hiding Indians
to emerge and reclaim their villages.
This would feed not only the Indians
but satisfy the starved Spanish need.
After discussing how to proceed
(for we knew no Indians in these parts)

we selected two from the Indians
who were captive in that camp.
They had accompanied Alcazar's men
when he first sent a band to meet
Dorantes, Castillo and our companions.
They therefore knew the high regard
in which we were held by those Indians
who recognised the power and authority
which we wielded across the land
due to the miracles that attended our travel
and the many cures we had performed.
To this pair we added three from Culiacan
that they together might address
those hiding in the jungle
and in the distant mountain villages.
While we awaited the Indians' return
the Governor attended to our care
making a present of his own clothes to wear.
For weeks I struggled to tolerate
the feel of cloth against my bare skin.
And none of us could lay in beds
sleeping more soundly on hard floors.

In two weeks the departed Indians returned.
With them walked the three chiefs
of those who hid in the mountains
and fifteen warriors to protect them.
The chiefs gave us emeralds and beads
along with the sacred feathers of eagles.
We bestowed on them the promise of peace
and the protection of the Prince of Peace.
Those from the river villages were not found
as fresh devastation by Alcazar's men
had persuaded them their best future
lay in decamping to distant territories.
I wish I could record that the Indians

welcomed our heart-felt entreaties
and descended en mass to re-occupy
their long abandoned homes.
The truth was that for many years
aggressive Christian avarice had devastated
the focus and rhythms of their lives.
And because our attitude and behaviour
differed so markedly from our compatriots'
they refused to connect our promises
with the hurtful Christian annexation.
We sought of them to put down their bows
and to live harmoniously, without warfare.
When they asked would we then ensure
the Christians did not attack and capture them
we directed the question to the Governor.
His response was to order Alcazar
to desist from further raiding.
He promised no raiding within his province
and to permit none to lock Indians in chains.
This intent was recorded by a notary
and signed by multiple witnesses.
Thus we made legal and obligatory
what otherwise relied on wavering
human memory, heart and trust.

θ θ θ

A full ten months passed between
our first meeting Christians
and our leaving for Mexico City
on the next stage of our journey to Spain.
But it was time we felt well spent
to ensure those we loved
would receive sound human succour.
It was no less than they deserved.
And no less than Spanish Christians

should in all solicitude provide.
The continued performance of that care
we entrusted to our new-found compatriots.
The success of that care is reflected
in the last adventure I here commit to ink.

21 The Glowing Jungle

EACH OF US on the day of our birth
owes life our certain death.
It is a fateful day we would ever delay.
Yet is not the moment our body dies
that same moment we are born in spirit
into the hidden kingdom we cannot know
except by casting off our entrancing body?
It is surely an instant of ecstatic revelation.
Yet we shrink from it as from an end.
Such thoughts come to me now
on contemplating not only my nearing death
but the final telling incident I would record.
It consisted of a death in life
that presages our life after death
in the mysterious realm we call Heaven.

As preface I observe my stay in Spain
made for bare and unhappy years.
After arriving at Seville's House of Trade
in late November of the year 1537
and despite my prior decade's privations
my taste for Spanish life did not return.
Indeed time in court proved a greater trial.
I know because I laboured fourteen months
to procure a ten minute audience
with the gracious King who ignored my speech
and chatted throughout to courtiers.
My goal was to lead an expedition
to harvest the New World's ample wealth.
I argued principally for agriculture
but acknowledged silver and gold

as lures necessary to fund a voyage.
My ill luck was Hernando de Soto
a renowned soldier and strategist
had been freshly appointed to lead
Spain's next New World expedition.
I was invited to second de Soto
but my months in Culiacan had filled me
of soldiers who knew much of arms
but little of what builds human links.
The King's advisors then presented me
an opportunity of unique promise.
The Governor of Rio de la Plata
had lately lost contact with his compeers
and it was suspected the province
was overrun now by hostile Indians.
A mission was required to locate him
and reinstall him in his prestige
or confirm he was dead and replace him
to govern Spain's newest province.
I would carry sole burden of leadership.
I saw this as a prime opportunity
to straighten the bent relation
of cohabiting Indians and Christians.

Ɵ Ɵ Ɵ

In March 1541 I arrived in Santa Catalina
an island off the coast of Portuguese Brazil.
I commanded four vessels and sufficient men
to plant new seeds of frontier fellowship.
I soon learned Santa Maria del Buen Aire
(being the new-built provincial capital)
had suffered waves of native attack
that breached and sacked the city
forcing the settlers to withdraw north
to the small inland town of Asunción.

We trekked west forty days from the coast
and found Asunción a flowering town
surrounded by newly planted fields
and well defended by troops and farmers.
It was there that I unhappily discovered
Governor Ayolas had been killed
during the relentless Indian warring.
I was proclaimed Lieutenant Governor.
There is no need to dwell at over-length
on how my command was undermined.
In truth the jungle and its inhabitants
proved immune to peaceful persuasion—
and the Christian settlers even less so.
But two issues were key to what transpired.

The first was Asunción's settlers
had accepted slaves from the Indians
and stolen native women from their homes
to act as servants, labourers and concubines.
I forbade such activity by decree.
The first casualties of my rule
were two noble men of the cloth
Franciscan friars of formidable appetite
who when advised fasting from the flesh
would now be their pre-Lent practice
declared they preferred Santa Catalina.
They then departed Asunción with six girls
placed in their care to become Christians.
I sent my soldiers to chase them down
a task their waddling progress made too easy.
The returned girls' parents rightly complained
not only were their children abused
but that the friars had preached
good Christian men took but one wife
yet here the Christian settlers took many.
Fairness, legality and Christian morals

required me to impound for trial
the two absconding Franciscan friars.
There was initial settler bristling at this
for they preferred to follow their own course.
But none else walked from Asunción.
Of greater consequence were the actions
initiated by Irala and his dark fraternity.
These men had established Asunción.
From the first they ruled it as their fiefdom.
Such rule included taxing their fellow settlers
along with the quelled local Indians
of one fifth of all their produce.
Dubbed the quinto, this tax was illegal.
Christian settlers paid in goods or currency
while from the unmonied Indians
Irala and his rapacious backers
accepted slaves to toil on their farms.
When I arrived those outside Irales' circle
promptly protested the qunito was theft.
I did my duty and applied Spanish law
forbidding the quinto's continued collection.
The initial response was complete silence.
But I had stirred dangerous intents.
I soon heard stifled murmurs
that Irala swelled with impatience
while the caged friars sang a vulture song
urging all those chafing I had crossed
to make a carcass of my command—
a revolt they licensed with churchly choirings.

It has been said to me I was naive to offend
those who had built new lives there.
I am not so naive as to believe
one may step into a box of vipers
without suffering painful bites.
Yet I have not survived so far

to quail before bullies, dissemblers, thieves.
Nor was I named Lieutenant Governor
to banquet at the table of corruption.
I took pains to deny Indian cannibalism
where they ate their cousins caught in battle
and had some success at civilizing them.
Yet the cannibalism of avaricious settlers
who joyfully feasted on their own
proved far more difficult to abolish.
The reward for my efforts
was to be dragged at midnight from my bed
and placed in that same cage
the freed friars had formerly occupied.
Legal depositions were filed
testifying to my unscrupulous practices
that showed Asunción's placid settlers
were so put in despair by my snatching
they had no choice but to imprison me.
Domingo de Irala cunningly held himself
from the machinery of this overthrow
and emerged the annointed civil ruler.
I remained a year in captivity
before I was shipped back to Spain
where outrages were performed on my name.
Yet I shall not dwell on those travesties
for all are but prologue to the last words
I choose to conclude this account.

ϴ ϴ ϴ

Soon after first reaching Asunción
on a sun-drenched sultry afternoon
I walked alone from the town
in search of refuge from contending men.
I strode the tilled fields where maize shoots
broke the dark loam-rich soil

and entered the jungle fringing the farms.
There I found that same quiet I often felt
when walking naked with my friends
as we traversed the New World lands.
This sense of solitude had deserted me
during my unhappy hiatus in Spain.
As I stepped through the undergrowth
the sounds of human living died
and I savoured the familiar grip of nature
as a tactile envelope of smells and sounds:
the mushroom odours of decaying leaves
the raucous calling of unseen birds
and the happy buzzing of excited bees
as they followed eddies of scents
then alighted on trembling flowers.
I paused near a shaded stream
and watched a pregnant doe
gently step between fallen trucks
then bend to bury her nose in fresh grasses.
With her I tasted the sweet shoots
she hungrily pulled at then chewed.
She lifted her head and her languid eyes
cast around before stopping on my form.
We stood some time in mutual regard
fallen deep into each other's eyes
as we shared a silent communion
of one living being to another.
Unhurriedly she turned away
pushed past vines that draped her passage
and moved deeper into the jungle.

I remained inwardly unmoving
immersed in life's cascading song.
Some say the language of nature
is a secret God locked into creation
that man might ever fruitlessly wonder at

to keep his swaggering self-pride in check.
I think of nature as a discourse
to which each life contributes a sentence.
But swept up in the tasks of human building
nature becomes a footnote to our living
and each person we know becomes
a fitfully recalled word we too soon forget
when life shreds and scatters it to the winds.
All this I speculate on now because
in the midst of that singing jungle
I found an unspoken language
that bloomed in perfect expression
and enthralled me with the wonder of what is.
The sun's beams filtered in a playful jumble
through the trees' branches and leaves
dancing off the stream's rippling surface
making that small clearing
wherein I was hushed and paused
the centre of the glowing world.
I stood transfixed and rapt.
An unusual feeling then fell on me.
It was as though a cloud
did pass not over but through me.
I then observed all buoyant life
and my every brooding care
was slowly sucked from my breathing body:
all my administrator's anxieties
all my obsessions with others' actions
all my need to defend my name
all I held close and that held me—
everything I tenanted dropped away.
I have often lived close to death
in blood-soaked battle
while crossing storming oceans
and in the sapping embrace of high fever
yet at no other time was I so convinced

as in that glowing jungle glade
that I would die within the minute.
I relaxed within and opened to what came.
Perhaps the heavenly realm we seek
shared an ecstatic sliver of itself
while I stood dying in that glowing glade.
For in that declining moment
my self's private constructs fell from me
and exposed not a nothing
but rather an inward presence
that glowed in harmony with the world.
I cannot explain it better than that.
I earlier recounted how in my travails
I lost my Old World status and clothes.
To that I now add the divination
that the range and weave of human life
is more than merely what we learn and know.
I felt myself reborn as a simple man
uncompounded of accustomed human clatter
but as something more than pen can capture.
As abruptly as the feeling arrived it lifted.
As the writing of this account attests
I did not die in that jungle.
I lived to return to the burdens of human life.
Yet I ever carry this new-born certainty in me.

Ɵ Ɵ Ɵ

So ends this headlong chronicle
of my singular adventures
in the lands we call the New World.
My life is no success in Spanish eyes.
Judgement of my failed governorship
was made by the Council of the Indies.
After five years of deliberation
in 1551 I was stripped of all my offices

and forbidden from setting foot
on any New World coast on pain of death.
I was then banished to serve the King
in the North African city of Orán
where I would perform my duties
at the cost of my own purse.
Poverty meant I possessed no purse
rendering this excessive edict moot.
It was rescinded within the month
and I was left to live my last days
far from my home town
in the ancient city of Seville.
Here I perform as an occasional scribe
to the unlettered and the unable.
I sit now in a room so small
I eat at my study desk and sleep on a bench.
Yet I have paper, pen, leisure and health
sufficient to record those exploits
that gave me no wealth and much suffering
but proved the making of me as a man.
I here praise God who made me what I am.
May my few remaining years not prove
a denial of all those that went before.